INTEGRITY IN EDUCATION
AND OTHER PAPERS

INTEGRITY IN EDUCATION
AND OTHER PAPERS

BY

GEORGE NORLIN ,*1871-1942*,

Essay Index Reprint Series

BOOKS FOR LIBRARIES PRESS
FREEPORT, NEW YORK

First Published 1926
Reprinted 1972

Library of Congress Cataloging in Publication Data

Norlin, George, 1871-1942.
Integrity in education; and other papers, by George Nor-
lin. Freeport, N.Y., Books for Libraries Pr. [1972]
231 p. 23 cm. (Series note)
(Essay index reprint series)
Reprint of the 1926 ed. Bibliographical footnotes.
CONTENTS:--Integrity in education.--Prometheus up-to
-date.--The religion of progress.--[etc.]
I. Title.
PS3527.O4515 1972   814'.5'2   74-177964
ISBN 0-8369-2568-8

PRINTED IN THE UNITED STATES OF AMERICA
BY
NEW WORLD BOOK MANUFACTURING CO., INC.
HALLANDALE, FLORIDA 33009

CONTENTS

INTEGRITY IN EDUCATION
AND OTHER PAPERS

INTEGRITY IN EDUCATION AND OTHER PAPERS

INTEGRITY IN EDUCATION

The French have a saying that "All generalizations are lies, including this one." This is a sound paradox which it is well for us all to bear in mind at all times, and especially when we allow ourselves to complain, as do many of us today, that we are living—and not too happily living—in an age of uneducated specialists. There are, of course, specialists and specialists. There are, for one thing, the specialists of our industrial order, of our factory system—mere bolts or rivets in a vastly complicated machine, repeating day after day and all day long the same narrow routine, condemned to see life in fragments and to live it in fragments, with little comprehension of the whole, with no integrating vision to give zest and meaning to their isolated tasks. These are growing alarmingly in number and threaten to become the prevailing type in our modern world.

Every gain of civilization has been purchased at a price. There was a wholeness—an integrity—of life in primitive society when men found their own food, manufactured their own clothing, built their own shelters, and were of necessity bound together by a common body of experience and knowledge, by a common vision, however limited, and by a common faith—there was then a wholeness of life which has now largely vanished from the earth, and which seems doomed more and more to be lost in the increasing division of labor and in the gradual dissociation of mankind. The genus *Homo Sapiens* is hardly distinguished any more by a common body of experience or knowledge. At least it is no longer bound together by its sapience but is, on the contrary, broken up by it. Man is being split up by his specialized attainments into an ever-growing number of species and sub-species, each shut off from the rest in some narrow cave of experience and knowledge, and having in common, besides his animal inheritance, a common impulse to escape from his work-a-day prison into a world of romance, a world of thrills—thrills of the movies, of the sensations of the printed page, of stepping on the gas and whizzing through space.

Perhaps it ill becomes us to quarrel with this fact; perhaps we should be thankful that men still find things to do and enjoy in common. Only we cannot dodge the question whether the superficial things which they now have in common are enough to hold society together, or whether deeper cohesive forces must be set at work if the structure of our industrial order is to stand.

Against this danger, which is by no means confined to our industrial life, we summon education to "come over and help us." But, unfortunately, education is itself drifting toward the same shoals; for in the academic world we are suffering a disintegration of learning and a disaggregation of scholars which is no less alarming than what is taking place in the world at large. There are, we gratefully acknowledge, exceptions to the rule; there are educators who try to view their tasks in relation to the whole situation; there are scholars who seek to grasp the significance of their specialties in relation to a larger unity of knowledge; there are scientists who "pluck the flower out of the crannied wall" and attempt to see in it and make others see in it "what God and man is"; there are men who still dream that the supreme task of the *Homo Sapiens* is the organization of the significant facts now scattered and even hidden away in isolated compartments of knowledge into a synthesis—a philosophy of life which men can live by.

But such men are now looked upon somewhat askance. There is a general suspicion, a common prejudice, which is entirely unwarranted, that broad scholarship is shallow and that the deeps of knowledge are sounded by minute measurements and tests carried on in fields so narrow and so isolated from each other that the one thing which intellectual workers may not have in common is fellowship in the intellectual life.

Now lest there arise a suspicion of loose speaking upon this matter, let us summon here as a witness a specialist known the world over for his researches in

a particular field. He writes: "With the development of our complex modern civilization, those individuals having the greatest intelligence tend more and
more to become specialists in comparatively narrow
fields. The professor of chemistry is not interested
in the details of biological work; even the professor
of literature may become so absorbed in the art of pre-
sentation as to forget the actual problems of life. The
biologist becomes an entomologist or a helminthologist
or even a coleopterist or a hematologist, and is bored
if anyone discusses a group of animals outside of his
particular province. The student of living forms often
will not look at their fossil ancestors, while the paleon-
tologist seems almost oblivious of the fact that his
subjects were once alive. All this is in a large measure unavoidable and it ill becomes anyone to complain
of the specialists, whose gifts to mankind can hardly
be overestimated. It is of course true that faculties
do not consist entirely of specialists, but the ablest
and the most experienced members are mainly of this
type. What do they have in common? Not much that
can be called intellectual; rather, the superficial things
of life, games and amusements, funny stories and light
conversation. * * * Let us put it this way: our
frivolities unite us; our intellectual labors separate us;
in the one field we speak a common language, in the
other we are increasingly unintelligible to one another.
* * * What can be expected of the students in the
presence of such a situation?" And he closes with
these impertinent words: "Could we only convert the

faculties, who knows what might happen to the students!"

This testimony may be summed up thus: Specialization has done great things for mankind and is therefore a good thing, but it is perhaps too much of a good thing when it results in a paradoxical state of affairs where an educational institution is a congeries of human beings who are dissociated so far as its purpose is concerned and associated only in the things which lie outside its purpose.

But let us supplement this testimony from another quarter. This time the witness is one who more than any other educator that we know of has insisted that education should embrace all of the relationships of human existence. He criticizes somewhat rancorously the professors of the sciences and of the arts in general because they do not envisage the whole of life in their culture. Outside of the narrow fields of their specialties, they are, he insists, less cultivated than their students; they are often lacking in self-discipline; they are sometimes boorish in their private relationships and commonly contemptuous and intolerant of the opinions of their fellows. They are, in a word, uneducated specialists.

"Whom, then, do I call educated?" he asks. "First, those who manage well the circumstances which they encounter day by day, and who possess a judgment which is accurate in meeting occasions as they arise and rarely misses the expedient course of action; next, those who are decent and honorable in their intercourse

with all men, bearing easily and good naturedly what
is unpleasant or offensive in others, and being themselves as agreeable and reasonable to their associates
as it is humanly possible to be; furthermore, those who
hold their pleasures always under control and are not
unduly overcome by their misfortunes, bearing up
under them bravely and in a manner worthy of our
common nature; finally, and most important of all,
those who are not spoiled by their successes and do
not desert their true selves, but hold their ground
steadfastly as wise and sober-minded men, rejoicing
no more in the good things which have come to them
through chance than in those which through their own
nature and intelligence are theirs from birth.   Those
who have a character which is in accord, not with one
of these things, but with all of them—these I maintain are educated and whole men, possessed of all the
virtues of a man."

This is a severe criticism of a piecemeal education as failing to produce the scholar and the gentle-
man in one; as failing above all in the ethical objectives of education: self-control, equanimity, courtesy,
sympathy and tolerance.   Perhaps it may be the less
offensive and the more acceptable to us for not having
been pointed at our time; for, whereas the first witness produced here is a professor of zoölogy [1] in an
American university, the second witness is an Athenian
schoolmaster [2] who exactly twenty-two hundred and

---

[1] Cockerell, in *School and Society*, April 26, 1924.
[2] Isocrates, *Panathenaicus*, 28-32.

sixty-seven years ago insisted that the supreme goal of life was the power "to see life steadily and see it whole," and that this was the supreme objective of education.

Now we have ventured to disturb the long repose of our ancient philosopher and pedagogue, not merely to show that the problem which is made by the natural tendency of man to shut himself within some narrow house is nothing new, but to speculate what this Athenian would think if he could be dragged from the little patch of earth and sea and the simple society in which he lived to face the vast complexity of the present world. He would find, no doubt, that man has advanced in the conquest of the material universe beyond what he would have dreamed that even the gods could do; that by his inventions he has not only opened up every nook and corner of the earth to his view, but has projected his gaze beyond the stars to grasp the infinitude of worlds beyond worlds; that he has devised vast mechanisms, educational, industrial, political—city mechanisms, state mechanisms, national mechanisms, and even world mechanisms—as instruments to further what is conceived to be the inevitable progress of mankind. He would see all this and more than this, and we can imagine how it would astound him and how it would at first expand his soul and exalt his mood. But when he turned his eyes upon the realm of the spirit he would, we fear, be filled with amazement of a different sort. Here he would gaze upon the havoc of a thousand battles, with no clear mark anywhere of a decisive victory; and should he recall the goal of living and of education as he defined it centuries ago, and as we must define it still, namely, self-control—obedience to a ruling principle of wisdom; equanimity—the conflicts of the soul composed in an enduring peace; the social virtues of sympathy, courtesy and tolerance, which spring from a mutual fellowship in the things of the mind and of the spirit— the things which distinguish man as man, he would find that towards this goal little advance has been made, if any progress whatsoever. He would find instead a world-wide spiritual unrest, a deep yearning of the mind, a great hunger for a philosophy of life, for an integration of the facts of human experience, of human knowledge, and of human aspiration, into a religion which is also a science or into a science which is also a religion, by which we may confidently order our lives and for which, if need be, we would gladly lay them down—a world-hunger which must feed upon itself, because we possess neither science nor religion, but only unreconciled fragments of science and religion.

And we can imagine that, seeing these things and feeling these things, he might experience some depression of his mood of exaltation, and might even be swept away upon the swelling tide of melancholy on which are drifting hither and yon the thinking men and women of this day.

> The Sea of Faith
> Was once, too, at the full, and round Earth's shore

Lay like the folds of a bright girdle furled,
But now I only hear
Its melancholy, long, withdrawing roar,
Retreating, to the breath
Of the night-wind, down the vast edges drear
And naked shingles of the world.

Ah Love, let us be true
To one another! for the world, which seems
To lie before us like a land of dreams,
So various, so beautiful, so new,
Hath neither joy, nor love, nor light,
Nor certitude, nor peace, nor help for pain;
And we are here as on a darkling plain
Swept with confused alarms of struggle and flight,
Where ignorant armies clash by night.

"Where ignorant armies clash by night!" How
many of us have tried to answer the question why it
is that the battles which are now waged among us between so-called science and so-called religion, or between what we would more accurately call fragmentary views of science and equally fragmentary views
of religion, dramatized not long ago in the trial of a
teacher in the schools of Tennessee, have singled out
this country as a unique curiosity among the other enlightened peoples of the world? Is it that we are less
enlightened than they? Or, since this intolerant warfare is carried on in a country which is served by a
greater number of churches, which is more abundantly
equipped with schools, public and private, which is
more thickly dotted with colleges and universities than

any other country under the sun, is it that we are in a fashion more educated than they? Is it that we are each of us possessed of some fragment of experience and knowledge, and, knowing this, think we know it all? Is it that a little learning is a dangerous thing, or, if we may paraphrase the saying, is it that a narrow learning is an intolerant thing? Is it, in fine, that we Americans, more than any other people, are a collocation of specialists, perhaps of uneducated specialists?

But, assuming that there may be some truth in these imaginings, what is to be done about it? Is there nothing that we can do about it? Are we, as it is commonly said, so caught up in the coils of an inexorable system that we cannot help ourselves? And is it true that protesting against it is like complaining of the weather—interesting, but purely academic and unprofitable? Well, we do in fact escape the extremes of weather in large degree by the kind of shelters which we build, and we may venture to believe that we can escape in large degree the dangers of over-specialization by the kind of schools which we build. It is, after all, a question of what we want to do and how much we want to do it.

We must recognize, of course, that our civilization is under a tremendous debt to the specialist, and that no scheme of education can be adequate for modern life which leaves this fact out of account. We need not, however, fear lest the demands of a specialized society for specialized training be neglected; they are so immediately pressing and insistent that they will always have at least the attention which they deserve, whereas the fundamental need of human beings to share in common a cultivated life is, like salvation, a thing easily put off to a more convenient time; and unless the high priests of learning are in season somewhat urgent in the matter there will be nothing left for them to do but to administer extreme unction.

It is the first business of public education to keep civilization alive; to hand on to each generation the significant achievements of past generations; to swing us into step with the forward strides of mankind, so that we, like the runners in the ancient torch-race, grasping the torch from the runner behind may speed it on to the runner ahead—a torch, mind you, not merely a vast accumulation of ill-assorted erudition locked away in the archives of our libraries, but a torch to light us on our way.

This we are now doing only in our dreams, and most of us are well aware of the immense difficulties of doing it in fact. The vast increase in the mass of knowledge, together with the disintegration of learning and the disaggregation of scholars and teachers, is against us. Nevertheless, we are not doing what it is humanly possible for us to do; for we may have faith that the ingenuity of man, which has mapped the complicated cosmos of the atom and measured the number of light-years to the most distant star, could, if devoted to this task, organize and integrate, within a reasonable compass, a common body of knowledge which would serve to make us feel at home in the two-fold world in which we have to live: the world of human relationships and the physical universe—a curriculum of training in the fundamentals of a common cultivated life. We should still have the problem of getting teachers for such an education, since at present we are trained to teach only parts of *ologies* and *isms,* but this, too, might in time be done, could we be sufficiently persuaded that it should be done.

Meantime, while we are groping for the way, perhaps it might help us if there could be blazoned in every school, in every college, in every university, the sacred admonition: "Where there is no vision the people perish"; and above all in the graduate schools of our great universities; for, whether we like it or not, these more than any other agency determine the course of education all along the line.

PROMETHEUS UP-TO-DATE

Those who knew the kindly Franklin K. Lane will always associate with him the whimsical statement which he gave out to his friends shortly before he died, in which he crowded his philosophy of life into two words: "I accept." He had in mind, I suppose, the familiar story about Thomas Carlyle. It will be recalled that when Margaret Fuller was quoted to him as saying, "I accept the Universe," Carlyle remarked sardonically, "Gad, she'd better!"

Now we all accept the universe in one sense or another—Gad, we'd better,—but we differ in our outlook upon it and in the temper of our acceptance. We may regard it in the last analysis as indifferent or even as hostile to our well-being, conceiving human life as an accident upon this planet or as a plaything of Destiny, accepting it, then, with reservation or with protest, like the Spirit of Pity in Thomas Hardy's epic drama *The Dynasts;* or we may, on the contrary, regard it as altogether friendly and admirable, accepting it, then, gladly and even with gusto—with three cheers, as it were, for the privilege of playing our parts on so excellent a stage. John Burroughs, for example, wrote a very interesting book, entitled *Accepting the Universe,* in which he quotes with approval his favorite

13

author, Walt Whitman, whom he regards as the most
inspired poet of Christendom:

> To breathe the air, how delicious;
> To speak, to walk, to seize something by the hand;
> To be this incredible God I am!
>
> .   .   .   .
>
> For I do not see one imperfection in the Universe,
> And I do not see one cause or result lamentable at last.

This is accepting the universe with a vengeance.
We cannot all go this length; most men have mixed
feelings about it; and some are out-and-out rebels
against its tyranny. Even Carlyle, with his "Gad,
she'd better," so far from accepting, revolts against
the acceptance of things as they are as a slave's philosophy. His *Freeman* fronts the universe—its moral
indifference and its cruelty—with an "Everlasting
No!"

There are, of course, times and moods in which we
can all join with Whitman and Burroughs in their
cosmic enthusiasm—when, for instance, on a day in
spring, the genial sun, the awakening earth, the swelling and budding everywhere about us, and the rising
tide of life within ourselves, all seem parts of one
worshipful mystery, chiming in unison: "God's in his
heaven; all's right with the world." But when, on the
other hand, we experience the destructive aspects of
nature—nature brutish and violent, "nature red in
tooth and claw with ravine"—we are not so easily
persuaded of the divine harmony of this universal

frame. John Muir is reported to have consoled his
friends in the California earthquake by the assurance
that it was only "Mother Earth trotting her children
fondly on her knee." But most of us may be par-
doned if in the face of like disasters we fail to be impressed by such marks of affection, seeking elsewhere
our refuge from "the pestilence that walketh in darkness, and the destruction that wasteth at noonday."

> Something within me aches to pray
> To some Great Heart, to take away
> This evil day, this evil day!
>
> ———
>
> Ha—ha! That's good, thou'lt pray to It:—
> But where do Its compassions sit?
>   Yea, where abides the heart of It?
>
> Is it where sky-fires flame and flit,
> Or solar craters spew and spit,
> Or ultra-stellar night-webs knit?
>
> What is Its shape? Man's counterfeit?
> That turns in some far sphere unlit
> The Wheel which drives the Infinite?
>
> ———
>
> Mock on, mock on! Yet I'll go pray
> To some Great Heart, who haply may
> Charm mortal miseries away.

The quest of the human intellect spinning cosmolo-
gies by the study fire has commonly been for some
First Cause of all things—some Primal Urge, some

Driver of the Infinite; but the quest of the human spirit bruised or broken on the wheel of life has ever been for "some Great Heart, who haply may charm mortal miseries away." In fact, struggling humanity, baffled by Fate, has never found it easy to accept the Universe. The ancient Hebrews tried to do so, seeking thus to justify the ways of God to man; and we, following them in our theology, have tried also, but with indifferent success. Job's cry to the power which rides the tempest and visits man with disease and affliction, "Though He slay me, yet will I trust in Him," has ever been a hard saying, especially to the Occidental mind.

Hardly anything of the sort is found in the writings of the Greeks. I say hardly; for late in the history of Greek civilization we find Marcus Aurelius exclaiming, "Whatsoever thou wishest, O Universe, I wish"; but the Stoic philosophy of acquiescence and resignation, of which this great emperor was a spokesman, was a thing apart in the thinking of the Greeks. They were, generally speaking, rebels against the inexorable decrees of what they called Fate—the cosmic law,—whether conceived as a power above that of the gods or identical with it. Stanley Baldwin, the prime minister of Great Britain, in a remarkable address before the last meeting of the British Classical Association, quotes Seneca's saying, "that a strong man matched with fortune is a sight for the gods to witness," and points out that this is the whole theme of Greek tragedy. "What was portrayed in the tragedy of the

Greeks," he says, "was nothing less than the human spirit at grips with the toils of destiny itself. * * * Always in their tragedies we are secure in the confidence that the characters will not prove unequal to the doom they have to bear. As it becomes more instant and inexorable, so their spirit becomes more indomitable to meet it, and it is never other than the mighty who are 'mightily laid low'."

Let me recall to you for a moment one of the most typical of these tragedies, the *Prometheus Bound* of Æschylus. Prometheus, the Titan, is here represented as the great lover of mankind. He found men existing wretchedly, like beasts in sunless caves, blindly ignorant and helplessly afraid. The instruments which could deliver them from this condition were in the hands of Zeus and the other gods; and the gods withheld their gifts. Prometheus stole fire from Olympus, brought it to man, and taught him the use of the arts, the securities, and the powers of the civilized life. For this he is punished by the gods— chained to a lonely cliff, taunted and tortured for his presumption; but, scornful and unyielding throughout the drama, he rises to a climax of defiance at the end, when the brute forces of nature are unloosed upon him and he is swept down in a cataclysm of destruction.

Now Prometheus in this play, the champion of mankind, is generally understood to be a poetic figure standing for mankind itself, and the tragedy is regarded as the first great picture in literature of man fighting his way slowly and painfully in the teeth of a hostile world, forcing from a reluctant nature the secrets of his own well-being, and gradually subduing to his own purposes the brutish forces which once enslaved him and even threatened to destroy him. In any case, Prometheus has been appropriated in our own day by evolutionary thought as a symbol of our conquest of nature through science and invention, and of our struggle to create a better world for men to live in—a personification of the idea of progress through human effort and sacrifice.

One aspect of this Promethean philosophy in our time is a grim materialism which accepts the whole drama of man as pictured by Æschylus, including the final catastrophe. For in spite of the cockishness of science in some quarters—the boast that man will put all things under his feet, even disease and death; that he will, as Mr. Wells puts it, one day "lord it over the stars," science itself in its sober moods commonly sets a final limit to the hope of human progress on this earth, warning us of the destined collapse of the material frame of things, when all our building must crumble into dust and all our striving shall end in nothingness. Lord Balfour has painted the depressing picture in his book *The Foundations of Belief:* "The energies of our system will decay, the glory of the sun will be dimmed, and the earth, tideless and inert, will no longer tolerate the race which has for a moment disturbed its solitude. Man will go down into the pit, and all his thoughts will perish. The uneasy consciousness which in this obscure corner has for a brief space broken the contented silence of the universe will be at rest. * * * 'Imperishable monuments' and 'immortal deeds', death itself, and love stronger than death, will be as if they had not been. Nor will anything that is be better or worse for all that the labour, genius, devotion and suffering of man has striven through countless ages to effect."

Bertrand Russell, with equal eloquence, sets forth the doom which in his belief must overtake all human striving in the eventual destruction of our cosmos. "That all the labours of the ages, all the devotion, all the inspiration, all the noonday brightness of human genius, are destined to extinction in the vast death of the solar system, and that the whole temple of man's achievement must inevitably be buried beneath the debris of a universe in ruins—all these things," he insists, "if not quite beyond dispute, are yet so nearly certain that no philosophy which rejects them can hope to stand. Only within the scaffolding of these truths, only on the firm foundation of unyielding despair, can the soul's habitation henceforth be safely built."

What he means by "unyielding despair," is explained at length in his essay entitled, *A Free Man's Worship*. According to his view, the business of man on this cosmic stage is, in a word, to play the man— to be Prometheus, snatching from eternal defeat such temporal victories as he can, "his head bloody but unbowed"; building amidst the blind chaos into which he is thrust his own temple of beauty and justice and love, as a refuge from the brutishness by which he is constantly beset and to which, at the tragic end, he must perforce succumb.

Happily so vivid a sense of impending doom as is bodied forth in this essay is out of the common. The end of this world, as predicted by materialistic science, is, after all, so vastly remote in time as to be for most of us a negligible prospect; and there are, moreover, reputable scientists to-day who venture to question whether it is a prospect at all. One turns, therefore, with some relief from the bitter melancholy of this mathematician-philosopher to the more robust, if not more consoling, Prometheanism of the Norwegian writer, Johan Bojer. His novel, *The Great Hunger*, deals with the tragic history of an engineer, whose incorrigible passion to remake the world brings his own world crashing about his head. Defeated in his dreams, abandoned by his friends, and reeling under the blows of circumstance, yet unbroken in spirit, he remains to the last a great lover and defender of humanity—a veritable Prometheus up-to-date. "We are flung," says this modern Prometheus as he makes his exit from the scene, "by the indifferent law of the universe into a life that we cannot order as we would; we are ravaged by injustice, by sickness and sorrow, by fire and flood. Even the happiest must die. In his own home he is but on a visit. He never knows but that he may be gone to-morrow. And yet man smiles and laughs in the face of his tragic fate. In the midst of his thraldom he has created

the beautiful on earth; in the midst of his torments
he has had so much surplus energy of soul that he
has sent it radiating forth into the cold deeps of space
and warmed them with God.

"So marvelous art thou, O spirit of man! So god-
like in thy very nature! Thou dost reap death, and
in return thou sowest the dream of everlasting life. In
revenge for thine evil fate thou dost fill the universe
with an all-loving God.

"We bore our part in his creation, all we who now
are dust; we who sank down into the dark like flames
gone out;—we wept, we exulted, we felt the ecstasy
and the agony, but each of us brought our ray to the
mighty sea of light, each of us, from the negro setting
up the first mark above the grave of his dead to the
genius raising the pillars of a temple towards heaven.
We bore our part, from the poor mother praying
beside a cradle, to the hosts that lifted their songs of
praise high up into boundless space.

"Honor to thee, O spirit of man. Thou givest a
soul to the world, thou settest it a goal, thou art the
hymn that lifts it into harmony; therefore turn back
into thyself, lift high thy head and meet proudly the
evil that comes to thee. Adversity can crush thee,
death can blot thee out, yet art thou still unconquerable and eternal."

All this is thoroughly Promethean. If there is despair in this view, there is no lying down in despair;
on the contrary, there is courage in it and a call to
arms. It will not do for the soft and flabby-minded;

but for stout hearts, there is a bracing tonic in this feeling which glorifies man and exalts him forever.

There is, however, another aspect of the Promethean philosophy which, though associated with the conquest of nature by human science, is really a perversion of the Promethean spirit, because, so far from making man out to be admirable, it tends to make him contemptible by dwelling on his insignificance in an ever-expanding universe. This has, of course, come in with the new cosmology. Sophocles, within the limited horizon of his time, could sing of man as the greatest marvel in a marvelous world. And even in the Middle Ages, when theologians sought to exalt the greatness of God by emphasizing the littleness of man, there still remained a degree of satisfaction in the belief that at any rate the earth was the center of all things—the footstool of the Almighty—and that man was the crown of creation, for whom the very stars were lit in the heavens, and the chief concern of God. Then came the Copernican astronomy and knocked all of man's conceit into a cocked hat. The earth is no longer the center even of our solar system, and is but a speck in a universe whose length and breadth and depth grows daily more immense. How then can the *All One* of this vast infinitude take thought of this negligible planet, or of this stumbling, shambling creature upon its surface which we call man? It is, in fact, not clear that the providence which modern science discovers in nature is more provident of man than of the centipede or of the boll-weevil or of the tubercle bacillus; indeed, there is a likely prospect that the insects and parasites will inherit the earth, unless we, the human kind, make a brave fight for it together instead of turning our weapons upon ourselves. The "gloomy Dean" of St. Paul's, who likes to poke fun at what he calls our "superstition of progress," warns us that "a microbe had the honor of killing Alexander the Great at the age of thirty-two, and so changing the whole course of history"; and that the microbes are still with us, and flourishing with unabated vigor.

But as if this were not enough, some of our self-styled realists would have us think of man, not in terms of the heights to which he has won or of those towards which his face is set, but of the depths from which he has crawled—ignoring Aristotle's admonition that "the nature of man is not what he was born as but what he is destined for," and insisting, on the contrary, that the reality underneath all of our aspirations—our philosophy, our poetry, our religion—is the primeval slime. I refer especially to the Freudian hypothesis, which its author developed to account for the actions of the mentally deranged, but which his less cautious popularizers, following Oscar Wilde's advice that nothing succeeds like excess, have exploited as a general philosophy of life. Emerson talked of the "enormous claims of the over-soul." These men chatter of the enormous claims of the under-soul—that submerged self of which we catch disconcerting glimpses in our troubled dreams; and nowadays the God whom we

must look to, if we are to be saved, is the *libido*—the
complex of our passions,—while the devil to pay, the
evil of our lives, lies in the frustration of desire.

Let nothing bind you:
If it be duty, away with it.
If it is law, disobey it.
If it is opinion, go against it.

There is only one Divinity: Yourself.
Only one God: You.

Beware that you worship no false idols,
Take no crust of manners or whimsical desires,
No surface-lusts and frailties,
For the real You hidden beneath.

But dig:
Dig with the shovel of will and engine of passion.

*   *   *   *   *

Dig down to self and set God free.

This poem—if it is a poem—is a fair sample of the
new gospel of expressionism, as it is termed; though
we should not go far wrong in characterizing many of
its developments as the deification of what the French
call *la nostalgie pour la boue,* our homesickness for the
mud.   It is, I have ventured to say, a perversion of the
Promethean philosophy—a pseudo-science which has
crept insidiously into our popular literature and our
common thought, obsessing us with the meanness and

futility of human endeavor and leaving us indifferent to the destruction of human life, whether by the inhumanity of nature or by man's inhumanity to man. Indeed this so-called realism tends to induce a cynical mood in which we accept war, not only as a business from which there is no escape, but as one which we do not care to escape; for war at any rate affords an opportunity to make our exit with some brave show of dignity from an unworthy existence.

What wonder that many are rising up in revolt against this counterfeit science—this bastard philosophy—, saying, "If this be science, we will have none of it?" The very revolt which we witness to-day, however one-sided it may be, is essentially Promethean in spirit—a protest of our self-respect, of our consciousness that the realities of human experience lie, not in the things which we share with the brute creation, but in the things which distinguish man as man, and that our progress is to be made, our salvation is to be won, not by indulging our homesickness for the mud, but by liberating what Lincoln called "the better angels of our nature."

We have not yet adjusted ourselves to the Copernican astronomy; we have not found our place in the immense new world which science is opening up. We are still in the wilderness stage; we are not even pioneers; we have only just begun to explore. But when we do find our place and our part, assuredly we shall not lack a Sophocles to hymn the dignity of man—nay, the divinity in man. For what, after all, has meas-

ured the number of light-years to the most distant
star? Man is himself creating the very immensity before which he now stands appalled! And even to-day,
when we have not yet found ourselves, it is in order
to sing:

Laugh and be merry, remember, better the world with a
    song,
Better the world with a blow in the teeth of a wrong.
Laugh, for the time is brief, a thread the length of a span,
Laugh and be proud to belong to the old proud pageant
    of man.

The Promethean view of life which we have considered up to this point is one according to which man
struggles alone against a hostile universe—against
"Fate" or "Necessity" or "the Gods," to use the Greek
terms, finding nowhere anything worthy of his worship save in himself alone. As the modern Job pictured in Mr. Wells' *Undying Fire* puts it: "And now
that my heavens are darkened, now that my eyes have
been opened to the wretchedness, futility and horror in
the texture of life, I still cling, I cling more than ever,
to the spirit of righteousness within me. If there is
no God, no mercy, no human kindliness in the great
frame of space and time, if life is a writhing torment,
an itch upon one little planet, and the stars away
there in the void no more than huge empty flares,
signifying nothing, then all the brighter shines the
flame of God in my heart. If the God in my heart
is no Son of any Heavenly Father, then is he Prome-

theus the rebel; it does not shake my faith that he is the Master for whom I will live and die. And all the more do I cling to this fire of human tradition we have lit upon this little planet, if it is the one gleam of spirit in all the windy vastness of a dead and empty universe."

This is the religion of humanism carried to the last degree. It may remind us of the story told by William James of the man who believed in No-God, and worshiped Him devoutly; but it is, nevertheless, a religion which is not without its faithful devotees. Man with his back to the wall, lost in a windy vastness, an itch upon a single planet, a disturber of the peace of the universe, an alien ever threatened with deportation, but fighting stubbornly to reclaim a bit of the wilderness of space for his proper habitation, is at least a heroic conception which appeals both to the soldier and the martyr in man. Yet we may be allowed to question whether it is not in reality a trifle too heroic; whether it does not too much savor of bravado; whether, in a word, it can serve for most of us as a working philosophy of life. If the truth as revealed by science constrained us so to think, we should no doubt make the best of it; but in truth no philosophy which seeks to envisage all of the facts of our knowledge and experience thus far can be said to condemn mankind to so bleak a prospect. The most militant evolutionist of them all, Thomas Huxley, in his historic lecture on *Evolution and Ethics*, himself has insisted in effect that while on the lower levels of creation brute force holds the stage, yet in the realm of the human struggle for a better life love is the fulfilling of the law. The avalanche crashing down the mountain-side belongs to one set of facts which may be explained by a principle of physics; the tiger in the jungle pouncing upon its victim belongs to a set of facts which may be explained by a biological principle; but Edith Cavell saying in the face of her executioners, "Standing as I do in view of God and Eternity, I realize that patriotism is not enough; I must have no hatred or bitterness toward any one," belongs to a different set of facts entirely which must be explained by a different principle entirely: and this principle, by which we seek to account for the mystery of humanity rising above everything that we know, including itself, may be termed the divine principle working in the life of man. Indeed there is a development of the Promethean philosophy which does not leave us battling alone in the universe, but rather allies the yearning heart of man with "some Great Heart" in the frame of things, some power beyond ourselves which makes for righteousness—a power which is not of the tempest or of the pestilence or of the indifference or violence of nature, but a divine spirit which strives for perfection in a world of imperfection, a divine partner with us in our struggles, the captain of our host. This is not a new idea, however heterodox it may be. It is as old as Plato and probably older. In modern times it has been set forth with elaborate clearness by John Stuart Mill, whose confident prediction, at the close of his essays on religion, that this idea is destined to control the religion of the future, is not without a degree of fulfillment in much of the thinking of the present day.

Much of the spiritual distress of the world, complains the Oxford physicist, Sir Frederick Soddy, comes from confusing divine with material force, or, to use his own words, "from enthroning God in the wrong place." This is dramatically brought out in Mr. Wells' war-novel, *Mr. Britling Sees It Through.* Readers of Mr. Wells will remember the mental ferment pictured in that book—the disillusionments, the horrors, the personal tragedies of the war obsessing the mind until reason is all but unseated; they will recall the mood of revolt against an All-Mighty who permitted all these things to be, and also the peace which settled upon Mr. Britling when the thought came like a new evangel that the god of theology was not, perhaps, the true God at all. "The theologians," says Mr. Britling, "have been extravagant about God. They have had silly absolute ideas—that He is all-powerful, that he is omni everything. But the common sense of man knows better. Every religious thought denies it. After all—the real God of the Christians is Christ, not God Almighty; a poor mocked and wounded God nailed on a cross of matter. Some day He will triumph. * * * But it is not fair to say that He causes all things now. It is not fair to make out a case against Him. You have been misled. * * * God is not absolute; God is finite. A finite God who struggles in His great and comprehensive way as we struggle in our weak and silly way—who is *with* us—that is the essence of all real religion."

This idea of a God who struggles with us in our struggles, helping us and helped by us in turn [1]—a religion of all good sportsmen, as it might be termed—is a favorite doctrine of Mr. Wells to which he recurs again and again. It is the whole theme of his *Undying Fire* and of his *God, The Invisible King.*

It is also an idea of one of our great Americans— the psychologist and philosopher, William James, who may be commended to our mentally anæmic age because of the sound sense and bracing tonic of his practical philosophy. I quote from his essay, *Is Life Worth Living?* "Truly, all we know of good and duty proceeds from nature; but none the less so does all we know of evil. Visible nature is all plasticity and indifference—a moral multiverse as one might call it, and not a moral universe. To such a harlot we owe no allegiance; with her as a whole we can establish no moral communication. * * * If there be a divine spirit of the universe, nature such as we know her, cannot possibly be its ultimate word to man. * * * Now I wish to make you feel that we have a right to believe

---

[1] Cf. a recent symposium by various scholars, published under the title *Science, Religion and Reality* (Macmillan), p. 181: "We coöperate with God for the redemption of the world. He is not suspended on high in a changeless Olympus, but lives, suffers and hopes with us. In this lies the profound truth of Christianity which made God descend in sacrifice for Man."

the physical order to be only a partial order; that we
have a right to supplement it by an unseen spiritual
order, which we assume on trust, if only thereby life
may seem to us better worth living again. * * * I
confess I do not see why the very existence of an invisible world may not in part depend on the personal
response which any of us may make to the religious
appeal. God, himself, in short, may draw vital strength
and increase of very being from our fidelity. For my
own part, I do not know what the sweat and blood and
tragedy of this life mean, if they mean anything short
of this. If this life be not a real fight, in which something is not eternally gained for the universe by success,
it is no better than a game of private theatricals from
which one may withdraw at will. But it *feels* like a real
fight—as if there were something really wild in the universe which we, with all our idealities and faithful-
nesses, are needed to redeem; and first of all to redeem
our own hearts from atheisms and fears. For such a
half-wild, half-saved, universe, our nature is adapted."

I have left William James to the last because, to
my mind, the Promethean spirit takes its finest form
in him. His philosophy summons mankind to cease
from waging war upon itself and to present a solid
front against its natural foes—to band together under
one Captain, He with us and we with Him, fighting
the good fight, with the weapons both of science and
of religion, against brutishness and violence, cruelty
and death, ugliness and disease, ignorance and super-

stition—in a word, against all the tricks and maneuvers of the common enemy of Man.

"These, then," he says, "are my last words to you: be not afraid of life. Believe that life *is* worth living, and your belief will help create the fact. The 'scientific proof' that you are right may not be clear before the day of Judgment * * * is reached. But the faithful fighters of this hour * * * may then turn to the faint-hearted, who here decline to go on, with words like those with which Henry IV greeted the tardy Crillon after a great victory had been gained: 'Hang yourself, brave Crillon: we fought at Arques and you were not there!' "

I have set forth these attitudes towards life with the hope that, whether they appeal to us as reasonable or not, they may at any rate help to set our own faces in the right direction. Each one of us is for himself in duty bound to cleave to that philosophy which best squares at once with his knowledge, his experience, and his highest aspirations—that philosophy, above all, which gives zest and courage to his instinct to fight a good fight. But we may venture to insist that no view of life in this cosmos can be in line with the truth which fails to ground itself upon certain facts of human experience that are embraced in the Promethean philosophy. Prometheus in Æschylus mentions among the benefits by which he delivered men from savagery that he "caused blind hopes to dwell among them." Dean Inge, in his Romanes Lecture on *The Idea of Progress*, after dashing many of the hopes of our blind wor-

shipers of progress, does near the end of his discourse
put a good deal of emphasis upon the unquenchable
hope of man. "The climbing instinct of humanity and
our discontent with things as they are," he says, "are
facts which have to be accounted for." Hope, as he
points out, played a great part in the early Christian
teaching. The first Christian poet, Prudentius, made
hope the characteristic which above all things distinguished man from other living creatures. Saint Paul
included it in the trinity of Hope, Faith and Love;
and later Christian philosophers added a fourth—
Truth.

And now abide these four: Hope, which rises up
out of all the tragedies of existence and out of all the
philosophies of despair, to defeat them; Faith, which
embraces both our instinct for perfection and our
courage to fight for it; Love, which not only Saint
Paul but all mankind have accepted as the greatest
thing in the world; and Truth—the passion to "follow knowledge like a sinking star beyond the utmost
bounds of human thought." These abide; they do not
die; they have survived all the buffets of adversity
throughout all the ages of human history. Whence
came they? Whither go they? "I want," says John
Burroughs, in the preface to his *Accepting the Universe,* "nothing less than a faith founded upon a rock,
faith in the constitution of things." Well, these are
as much in the constitution of things as anything; they
are, themselves, cosmic forces to be accounted for, or
at any rate to be reckoned with; they are at least as

real as the Rocky Mountains or the force of gravitation, and who shall say that they are not as enduring? Nay, it is quite possible that even though the mountains pass away, and the earth and the moon and the sun, these things shall not pass away.

THE RELIGION OF PROGRESS

In the thought and in the literature of the last few years there is a strong current of misgiving about the future—a feeling that civilization has missed the way and that we are approaching a dark age.

This misgiving is, of course, not a new thing in history. Again and again in the past it has been voiced by the philosophy of disillusionment only to arouse mild interest in academic circles; but since the Great War, the question whether or not human society is headed in the right direction has been pressed upon our thoughts so insistently and so generally that it has become of supreme practical importance. For one of the great incentives prompting us to do our best and one of the great forces working for the betterment of the conditions of human existence is the feeling that in all our worthy striving we are building not for ourselves alone but for generations yet to come. Indeed, there is no truer measure of our culture, of our civilization, than the extent to which we project ourselves into the future. The animal takes thought only for the moment; the savage takes thought only for the day; the politician orders his life on the principle that the unborn have no votes; but the civilized man is concerned, not only for himself and for his children, but for his children's children's children.

The idea of progress as we think of it—the idea of the gradual and limitless march of humanity towards a more perfect state—is a growth of modern times. The ancients did not have it. They commonly thought of the present as representing a fall or a decline from some happy Eden or golden age; or if at times they entertained the thought of progress from a condition of brutish helplessness to one of civilization, as did Æschylus in his drama *The Prometheus Bound* and Lucretius in his epic *On the Nature of the World,* they thought of that progress as bounded by definite limits —of civilization as containing the seeds of its own inevitable decay, of the vast architecture of the world as doomed to crash one day in universal ruin.

> The cloud-capped towers, the gorgeous palaces,
> The solemn temples, the great globe itself,
> Yea, all which it inherit, shall dissolve,
> And, like this unsubstantial pageant faded,
> Leave not a wrack behind.

Such an outlook left little room for anything but a melancholy fatalism. Life was held a precious thing; there was a keen, almost a fierce joy in the light of the dear sun; but ever in the background lowered the dark shape of *Moira,* of inexorable Doom, pointing to the limitations of human life and the ultimate futility of human endeavor. And, generally speaking, the best that ancient religion or ancient philosophy could counsel was a mood of patient equanimity, of stoical resignation to the decrees of Fate.

Then came the new evangel into what Saint Paul called a world without hope—a religion of hope, of faith and of love. But as this religion crystalized into institutions, into cults, into the great establishment of the Church, this hope ceased to concern itself with the present world and projected itself into a world to come; this faith centered itself no longer on the possibility of a kingdom of God on earth, but upon the reality of an invisible, eternal existence; and this love came to be conceived as something which could be realized only in some heaven above the heavens.

Throughout the history of the Medieval Church and of the Medieval Age there is little or no thought of progress in our sense of the word, no thought of the gradual improvement of our life on the earth, no concern save to deliver mankind from "the world, the flesh and the devil" into the life to come. Earthly existence was disparaged as in itself mean and worthless, and hope built its castles beyond the grave.

The Renaissance marked a reaction toward a saner view of the power of man's intellect and of the value and dignity of life on this earth, and so prepared the way for our modern habit of thinking. But the idea of progress as it is popularly held to-day is hardly older than some who are now living. It is a birth of the great advancement of science and of engineering in recent times, of the use of coal and iron and steam and electricity, of the so-called industrial revolution, which during the single century which has passed since the day of Napoleon, and largely during our own generation, has wrought an infinitely greater change in the circumstances and conditions of human life than is to be found in the thousands of years of recorded history before Napoleon's time.

Of all the changes which this revolution has caused, the most radical change is in our conception of man's place in nature. Our conquest of nature—our rapid subjection of the very elements to our use and to our will—has delivered man from his oppressive sense of slavery to the blind forces of a hostile world and enthroned him, in his own imagination, upon the footstool of the Almighty.

"Die happy," said the Greek poet, Pindar, to one who had received the crown of victory in the Olympic games—symbol of the most enviable achievement of ancient life—"Die happy, thou canst not climb the brazen heaven." Here speaks the old-world sense of human limitations; only the gods could climb the brazen heaven. But we have mastered, we think, the secrets of the gods. We can climb the brazen heaven. We soar above the earth faster and to greater heights than the eagle; we plunge into the depths of the ocean where no fish can follow. We have in a degree conquered the earth, the sea, and now the air; we have in a degree conquered the limitations of space and of time; and these are but the beginnings of what we confidently expect to do. We set no bounds to our audacity. Intoxicated by the advances which we have made in biology and medicine, we dream of discoveries which may arrest the processes of decay in the living organism, prolong indefinitely the period of human life, and even perhaps deliver us from the doom of our mortality. One of our great engineers, also the President of a unique American college, has recently published what may be called his confession of faith in limitless human progress. Undaunted by the uncomfortable, although remote, prospect of the end of all human endeavor on this planet when the earth shall become as cold and lifeless as the moon, he suggests that long before this mundane climate shall become too severe for us, human science and engineering will have invented some machinery of transit by which we can journey hence at will and pick and choose our habitation among the stars. Shades of the Greek moralists! We could depart no further from their injunction that it behooves mortal men to think mortal thoughts.

Belief in progress is first set down as an article of faith, almost as a religion of consolation, in Tennyson's *Locksley Hall.* That was published in 1842. Nine years later, in 1851, there was held the great world-exposition in London—a central and spectacular demonstration of the marvelous achievements of science and invention, of the great material prosperity which they had ushered in, and of the general goodwill which then seemed to possess the nations of the world. In the literature of the time, in the address of the Prince Consort opening the exposition, in the leading articles of the journals of the day, in the verses of the poet laureate, there swells a chorus of gratulation on living in a wondrous age, of optimism for the future, and of faith that mankind had set its course in the direction of that "one far-off divine event toward which the whole creation moves."

In that same year, Herbert Spencer began the publication of his memorable writings, which extended the law of evolution to human society and asserted the perfectibility of man, not as a possibility merely, not merely as a goal towards which we may strive, but as inevitable in the very nature of things, as the effect of a cosmic urge impelling us, no matter what we do, onward and forward toward the ideal state. "Always toward perfection," he says, "is the mighty movement, towards a complete development and a more unmixed good."

This neo-fatalism of Herbert Spencer, bringing the support of science and philosophy to the exuberant hopefulness of the time, took possession of the popular imagination and became increasingly a sort of lay-religion. Some misgivings are expressed here and there, as in Tennyson's *Locksley Hall Sixty Years After,* but these are but passing shadows in a complacent age. Indeed, about the time when Tennyson wrote this reactionary poem, Frederic Harrison delivered his historic address on the *New Era,* in which he announced, apparently to an approving world, that the faith in the progress of humanity had taken the place of the hope of celestial rewards of the individual soul. And this faith remained unchallenged until the cataclysm of the World War.

What happened in that war—the most cruel, the

most horrible, the most disastrous war of recorded history; and even more what has happened since its close: the appalling increase of friction everywhere; of friction in every human personality—the acute accentuation of the world-old warfare in the soul of man, leading to deeds of recklessness and desperation, to the increase of crime and suicide; of friction in the home—the breaking up of family life, the increase of divorce; of friction between classes, between employers and employed; of friction between nationalities—the blazing forth of racial prejudices and hatreds throughout the world—all this has staggered our optimism and laid low our lofty dreams.

Perhaps the greatest shock of all has been the disconcerting revelation that our inventions may so easily be turned to our destruction, and that the very instruments of progress may be used to plunge us backwards towards chaos. The old oppressive sense of our limitations has surged back upon us in high flood, and now once more we ask the question of the Psalmist, though not in his grateful mood, "What is man that thou art mindful of him or the son of man that thou visitest him?"

We are disenchanted with our civilization; we see signs of its breaking down; and we are beginning to fear that it may go the way of the great civilizations of the past. Doubtless many to whom the whole trend and meaning of life are summed up in a Babson forecast or in the news that a speed record has been broken still persist in a swaggering optimism, but sober-minded men, the leaders of our scientific and philosophical thought, are expressing grave concern at the drift of human affairs.

A great churchman and a great scholar, Dean Inge, in a brilliant essay on *The Idea of Progress* has attacked with caustic and conclusive logic what he calls the superstition of progress—the Spencerian doctrine of a law of nature, a cosmic force impelling us inevitably toward perfection; but he goes further than that and finds in the conditions of the present grounds for the ancient view that every civilization contains the seeds of its own decay and dissolution.

A great physicist, Sir Frederick Soddy of Oxford, speculating in his book which he calls *Science and Life* on the possibility of discovering the key to release the store of tremendous energy now locked in the atoms of matter—a form of energy so great that could we command it at will we would be able to transform the earth into an Eden or blow it to smithereens at our pleasure—hopes that this discovery may not be made in our time, because he thinks that in our present state of intellectual and moral barbarism we would probably use this power to blow things into smithereens.

A great anthropologist, Doctor Flinders Petrie, has published a book called *The Revolutions of Civilization,* in which, discussing the rise and fall of the civilizations of history, he points out that the first symptoms of decline are the uprising of the mob and the decadence of art, leaving us to draw such inferences as we like from the spread of the dictatorship of the proletariat in modern society and from the surrender of our taste to a kind of music which reproduces all the rhythm and all the lilt of an elevated train.

An able sociologist, Doctor Austin Freeman, in a searching work called *Social Decay and Regeneration,* draws a very disturbing picture of our machine civilization—the mechanization of human life, its piecework monotony, the growing enslavement of man to his own inventions. The discoveries of modern science and their applications have, in his view, entangled mankind in the coils of the appalling complex which we call our industrial civilization—that monstrous world-machine which has become so interrelated in all its parts that a dislocation in one quarter results in universal disorder; which has grown so complicated and involved that it is beyond our power to understand it and beyond our skill to control it; which has gained such enormous momentum that we cannot check it or direct it as we would; which did in fact break utterly from our control a few years ago and wrought such world-wide havoc that we cannot even now reckon up, to say nothing of repairing, the damage; and which may in the end, unless in the meantime there is effected some heroic advance in human engineering, overrun and crush us all.

Finally, a great psychologist, Professor William McDougall, who has recently been called to this country to carry on the high traditions of the department made famous by William James, has delivered a series of lectures now published in book form under the title,

Is America Safe for Democracy? That this title is something more than a rhetorical question appears from his prefatory words: "As I watch the American people speeding gaily with invincible optimism down the road to destruction, I seem to be contemplating the greatest tragedy in the history of mankind. Other nations have declined and passed away and their places have been filled, the torch of civilization has been caught up and carried forward by new nations emerging from the shadow-land of barbarism. But if the American nation should go down, whence may we expect a new birth of progress?"

The only optimistic voice now strong enough to be heard over the world is that of H. G. Wells; and his admonition that "history is a race between catastrophe and education" has little in common with the blithe and careless fatalism of the Victorian Age.

Now this deluge of misgiving and of warning in the literature of our day, of which I have mentioned here only a few significant types, is a good thing for us if we do not allow it to sweep us off our feet. It is a good thing for us if it arouses us to take stock of ourselves and see whither we are drifting. It is a salutary thing for us if it brings home to use the utter folly of measuring human well-being in terms of material prosperity and power to the neglect of progress in the spirit and soul of man.

It would, however, be equal folly to lay our distresses and our shortcomings, as some have done, to the diabolical influence of science and invention, and to propose, as some have done, to throw away our machines and return to primitive conditions of life. Our great scientists have lived and worked with a disinterestedness and a consecration which are unsurpassed among all those who have spent themselves in the service of God and man. And it is, we may believe, upon the broadening of science to include all the problems of human existence—of a consecrated science, a science which is also a religion or a religion which is also a science—that we rest our hope of a better order.

It is as unfortunate as it was perhaps inevitable that scientific inquiry should have concerned itself hitherto so largely with the mysteries of the material world and so little with the mysteries of man and of human society. Aristotle in his day published treatises upon physics and chemistry which now seem utterly fantastic, they are so hopelessly out of date. But, as Professor Robinson has pointed out, he also wrote books on ethics and politics which are still standard works in their field. In our knowledge and practice of the laws of the physical universe we are living in the twentieth century; in our knowledge and practice of the principles which govern the world of man and of human relationships we are living two thousand years ago.

We are suffering from a one-sided development, from disharmony, from maladjustment; we are out of joint with the times. We have gone forward during the last hundred years, especially in the last quarter century, with incredible rapidity in our mastery over the forces of nature, but very little if at all in our mastery over ourselves. We have advanced tremendously in material power, but very little if at all in power of intellect or of moral responsibility. We have developed engines with little thought to the steering gear or the controls. The vast and infinitely complicated machinery of the present-day world demands of us the mentality and wisdom of supermen, whereas our psychologists tell us that we are most of us of the mental stature of thirteen years. We are like children playing with fire or like savages toying with dynamite.

In 1878, Alfred Nobel, a Swedish chemist, discovered cordite, one of the most powerful of modern explosives, and was rewarded with great riches. As if alarmed at the potential danger which lay in his invention, he invested his fortune in a foundation for the good of humanity, including a foundation for the promotion of peace. But the discovery of cordite and other discoveries which followed in its train made possible the unique horrors of the late war.

Now if this episode may be said to be representative of modern history, if it is typical of the trend of our life today; if we continue to indulge first of all our appetite for power, and only occasionally, and then as an after thought, to bethink ourselves of the good of humanity, we may well ask ourselves the sober question: What force, as things are now going, is likely to have its way with us, cordite or the Nobel peace prize?

We shall, of course, continue in our quest of power;

we shall go on inventing more and still more machines; but surely after the revelations and the heart-searchings of the past few years we cannot now be guilty of the blind stupidity of not seeking first of all to redress the balance between material power and spiritual power; of not building up and strengthening first of all those agencies and institutions of education and of religion which recognize the supreme value of human life and the supreme importance of developing greater men and greater women—stronger material to bear the increasing stresses of our modern world.

I recall from somewhere a Roman saying: *Ubi nihil timetur, quod timeatur nascitur.* If in this day we do well to give our thoughts to the misgivings of thinking men, it is because a blind optimism is quite as inimical to our true progress as a blind despair. But of all times this is no time for us to take things lying down. If Mr. Wells is right in saying that history is a race between education and catastrophe—and one may believe that this voices a sober optimism,—then this great hope is a fair challenge to the soldier which is in every one of us seeking a cause worthy of his courage. There is no cosmic urge impelling us, no matter what we do, towards perfection any more than there is a cosmic force driving us, in spite of ourselves, downward to destruction. Evolution, so far as human society is concerned, is in our hands to direct and determine. The Kingdom of Heaven is not outside of ourselves but within us, and whether we help to bring it to pass depends upon what we think and say and do.

For there is in our nature something which is quite as real as any cosmic force, something which we may think of as God in us, an instinct for perfection, a discontent with things as they are, a desire to leave the world better than we find it, which we may safely take to be our guide—our pillar of fire by night and our pillar of cloud by day.

ETHNOLOGY AND THE GOLDEN AGE

It is the common habit of civilized peoples to assume that the fabric of their customs and institutions represents a departure from a primitive condition or state of nature, and to estimate the value and direction of their mode of life by the contrasts which it presents to the days of long ago. But the picture which is drawn of this state of nature is itself colored in no small degree by the prejudices of the moment either for or against present conditions and tendencies. Those who are intoxicated by the wine of their achievements are prone to think of the natural state as the negation of all the good things which man has won for himself in the course of an ever-forward march, while those who have grown oversensitive to the evils of civilization dream of a lost paradise or a golden age.

But in seeking to understand these antithetical points of view we have to reckon with something more than subjective mood or fancy. Culture theorists of the more sober sort have usually sought some basis of historical reality, some solid ground of fact; assuming that in distant parts of the world, far removed from the currents of civilization, people remain very much now as they were in the beginning,[1] they have com-

[1] As Vilhjálmur Stefánsson assumes that he found among the Dolphin and Union Straits Eskimos the conditions of the Stone Age: "My Quest in the Arctic," *Harper's Magazine*, CXXVI, 512.

monly taken as their points of departure, in tracing the
course of human development, facts or reported facts
about far-away primitive tribes.   Professor J. L.
Myers in a recent pamphlet [2] has presented a careful
study of the influence of ethnology on modern political
science, proving, especially for the seventeenth and
eighteenth centuries, that there is a very close relation
between the shifting ideas of that period as to the
origin and growth of society and the ever-increasing
store of information about uncivilized peoples which
was opened up by exploration of remote regions of the
earth, especially the Americas.   The first accounts of
primitive life, derived from discoverers who brought
to these aborigines "not peace but a sword," [3] led
to the view of man in his natural state which we
see in Shakespeare's Caliban and Hobbe's wretched
creature "poor, nasty, and brutish, in continual
fear and danger of violent death"—a conception
which held the boards until the Jesuit Fathers,
approaching the Indians as human beings like themselves, and not seldom meeting with response of docile
affection and loyalty, began in their letters home
to contrast the simple virtues of these children of
nature with the vices of European civilization, and
so prepared the way for the ideal savage of Pope and
Rousseau. [4]

[2] *The Influence of Anthropology on the Course of Political Science,*
University of California Press, February, 1916.
[3] Myers, p. 2.
[4] Lavisse, *Hist. de France,* VIII, 2 Partie, p. 308: "Avant lui [Rous-
seau], les missionares jésuits du Paraguay avaient écrit des *Lettres*

We have here, if I am not mistaken, an instructive parallel to the influences which determined the course of *Culturgeschichte* in ancient Greece. When the Hellenes established the outposts of their civilization among the hostile tribes which bordered the Mediterranean, and especially on the coasts of what they at first called the "Unfriendly Sea," they must have seen in the savage life which opposed and threatened them mainly the dark obverse of their own brighter culture.[5] Their tales of cave-dwelling, man-eating monsters reflect something of this early experience;[6] and as late as Herodotus we find the tendency to dwell, by way of contrast, on the savage customs of the non-Greek world,[7] notably of the northern barbarians.[8] It was inevitable that the Greeks should think of such revolting practices as human sacrifice and cannibalism, which they found still existing among uncivilized peoples,[9] as survivals from a primitive condition which they in their forward progress had left behind them, and that they should look on Hellenism, especially in the years before the first flush of their triumph in the Persian Wars had faded, as embodying all that was best in human

où ils opposaient les vertus de leurs catéchumènes aux vices des civilisés, et répandu en Europe des préjugés sur la supériorité de l'homme sauvage."
[5] See arguments drawn by geographers like Apollodorus from the term Ἄξενος, in Strabo vii. 3. 7; and Gilbert Murray's "Greece and the Progress of Man" in *The Rise of the Greek Epic*.
[6] Berard, *Les Phéniciens et l'Odyssée*, II, 175, 245; Maine, *Ancient Law*, p. 120.
[7] See especially iii. 38; and Bury, *Ancient Greek Historians*, p. 44.
[8] Book iv.
[9] Herod. iv. 103, 106; Pseudo-Platonic *Minos* 315 B.

achievement.[10]   The issue of that conflict was, indeed,
the final vindication of a mode of life which had been
till then by no means unprecarious.   In Athens, above
all, the past misgivings and hesitations to which the
pages of Herodotus bear ample witness now gave way
to that exaltation of spirit and confident pressing forward to the future which ushered in her Golden Age; [11]
and so, perhaps, it is no accident that Aeschylus, who
fought at Marathon and wrote the *Persae*, was, so far
as we know, the first Greek to bring into clear relief
the idea of human progress from a helpless, brutish
existence to the arts of life,[12] or that Sophocles, who
as a boy had led the victory chant after Salamis, was
inspired to hymn the marvelous conquests of man over
the blind forces of a reluctant world.[13]

Henceforth the deliverance of man from savagery to
civilization by the grace of Prometheus, or Palamedes,
or by his own upward striving becomes a recurring

[10] So in Euripides, *Orestes*, κοινὸς Ἑλλήνων νόμος (495), saves the
world from the brutish violence of barbarism:

τὸ θηριῶδες τοῦτο καὶ μιαιφόνον
παύων, ὃ καὶ γῆν καὶ πόλεις ὄλλυσ' ἀεί (523, 524)

Cf. Dümmler, *Prolegomena zu Platon's Staat*, pp. 47-49.
[11] For the psychological effects of the defeat of Persia, see Arist.
Pol. 1341a. 30; Diodorus 12. 1. 3, 4.
[12] *Prom. Bound*, 462 ff.   Xenophanes anticipates Aeschylus in a
brief couplet:

οὔτοι ἀπ' ἀρχῆς πάντα θεοὶ θνητοῖσ' ὑπέδειξαν
ἀλλὰ χρόνῳ ζητοῦντες ἐφευρίσκουσιν ἀμεῖνον

Frag. 18 in Diels *Frag. der VorSokratiker*.   The idea of improvement
in human conditions was, of course, implicit in culture-hero myths;
It may possibly have been a part of epic tradition, but the dating
of the Homeric Hymn to Hephaestus is pure guesswork.
[13] *Antigone*, 332-64.

theme of the Athenian drama.[14] The latest example
of it in the tragic poets is a fragment of Moschion [15]
where we are well on the way to the organic development theory [16] of the fifth book of Lucretius:

> Time was when mortals lived the life of beasts
> And dwelt in mountain grots and sunless caves;
> For sheltering houses they had none as yet
> Nor spacious city strong with masoned towers.
> No curving plows then broke the swarthy glebe,
> The nurse of corn, nor pruning iron bestowed
> Its care on teeming rows of vines; but Earth
> Was waste and barren, yielding up no fruit.[17]
> Men fed on human flesh by slaughtering men;
> And Law lay prostrate; Violence sat the throne
> With Zeus; the strong devoured the helpless weak.
> But soon as Time, which brings all things to birth
> And fosters all, had wrought again a change
> In human life, whether by lending them
> Prometheus' wit or sheer Necessity
> Or Nature's self, through long experience,
> To be their guide, divine Demeter's gift
> Was found, a gentle sustenance; and found
> Was also Bacchus' pleasant spring; the land,
> Unsown before, was plowed by spans of oxen;
> Cities now they girt with walls and houses built,
> And changed their savage life to gentle ways.
> Thenceforth the law enjoined to hide the dead

[14] Nauck, *Trag. Graec. Frag.*, pp. 59, 236, 542, 771, 931; Eur. *Suppl.*
201 ff.; Meineke, *Poet. Com. Graec.*, pp. 706, 707.
[15] Nauck, p. 813.
[16] Benn, *Greek Philosophers*, II, 99.
[17] Reading κοὺ τροφὴν φέρουσα.

In tombs and give to the unsepulchered
Their due of dust, and not to leave exposed
Reminders of their former ghastly feast.[18]

Moschion's sketch dates probably from the fourth century, but, although the notion of progress upward from savagery recurs in this period and later,[19] it is especially characteristic of the pride of achievement and buoyant optimism which followed the Persian Wars.[20]   Toward the end of the fifth century there is a marked cooling down of enthusiasm for things as they are [21] and, from this time on, an increasing disenchantment, a growing conviction, indeed, that civilization has lost the way; that it represents an aberration, a παρέκβασις, from the right path; and that, after all that may be said for the present mode of life, its

[18] It is significant that every detail of this picture of primitive savagery may be supplied from the wild tribes described by Herodotus in his fourth book: The Troglodytes dwell in caves and are in other ways little removed from animality (183); the Scythians have no walled cities or fixed abodes (46); nor do they plow (19); the Androphagoi are the most savage of human creatures; they are without restraint of any principle of right or law, and feed on men (106).

It is, of course, not necessary to assume that Moschion took his colors directly from Herodotus; the essential point is that such details of ethnology were available in the fifth century and probably earlier.   Gomperz, *Griechische Denker*, I, 312 (also Dümmler, *op. cit.*, p. 28), derives Moschion's sketch directly from Protagoras' Περὶ τῆς ἐν ἀρχῇ καταστάσεως, but Protagoras may have been indebted to Herodotus, perhaps "talked with him about ethnology at Thurii" as Gomperz fancies (I, 353); cf. also, Nestle, *Herodot's Verhältnis zur Philosophie und Sophistik*, pp. 17, 18.

[19] See Isocrates *Panegyricus* 28; Aristotle *Pol.* 1269 A 5; Diodorus i. 8; Delphic Inscription in *Bulletin de Corr. Hellenique*, 1900, p. 96; and Rohde, *Der griechische Roman*, p. 217.

[20] Gomperz, I, 311, 312.

[21] The afterglow of the triumph over Persia lingers fifty years according to Diodorus xii. 1. 3, 4.

outstanding facts are greed, luxury, and man's inhumanity to man.

This reaction of feeling is strikingly instanced in the disposition of the philosophers, beginning with Socrates, to hold aloof from political life and to live more and more in the realm of the ideal,[22] and, above all, in the cry, "Back to Nature," which became the dominating idea of the Cynics and, after them, of the Stoic school for centuries. Nature is now no longer "red in tooth and claw with ravine," but is the wise teacher and sure guide which erratic society has ignored or contemned; and the natural man is no longer the savage "nasty and brutish," but a simple and kindly being, having but little and that little in common with others, and with that little content; and he is to be found only in a far-away past, a Hesiodic Golden Age, or in a far-away present which civilization has not touched and spoiled.

Such reversions to Hesiodic pessimism were evidently in the air before the fifth century closed.[23] Perhaps they start with the Sophist Hippias whom Gomperz regards as the precursor of the Cynics and Stoics.[24] At any rate, they are reflected in Plato,[25] who, in certain moods, associates the virtues of temperance and justice with primitive conditions of a by-

[22] Plato *Rep.* 496 D, E.

[23] Pherecretes' Ἄγριοι seems to have been a burlesque on already current idealizations of uncivilized life. Plato *Protag.* 327 D; see Nestle, *op. cit.*, p. 27.

[24] *Griechische Denker*, I, 348.

[25] Barker, *The Political Thought of Plato and Aristotle*, pp. 151, 190.

gone age. In the *Laws* [26] he pictures the early state of
society as one of pastoral simplicity where all have
enough to satisfy their necessary wants, but none is
rich or poor, and so there is no occasion for envy or
insolence or injustice to arise. In another passage of
the same dialogue [27] he refers to the view that, of old,
men lived on the fruits of the earth, abstaining from
flesh in Orphic fashion; and in the *Republic,* in which
Socrates sketches the origin of a city in a state of
health, he prescribes a diet exclusively vegetarian—
bread and cakes and fruit spread out on the grass;
the people reclining on boughs of myrtle and yew,
wholesomely enjoying the frugal fare and each other's
pleasant company, sound of limb and long of life and
transmitting to their children an idyllic existence like
their own. To this Glaucon objects that Socrates
would not do differently if he were prescribing for a
community of swine, and insists that people should
live in a civilized manner with couches and tables and
the dishes and desserts of a modern bill of fare. "Very
good," says Socrates, "we are considering, it seems, not
the growth of a healthy city merely, but of a city luxurious and inflamed. I dare say it is not a bad idea, for
thus we shall discover the rise of justice and injustice." [28]

[26] 679 A-E; cf. 713.
[27] 782 A-D.
[28] *Rep.* 372 B-E; and Adam's Commentary; cf. Myers, *Herodotus
and Anthropology,* p. 163. But Plato does not commit himself to
this point of view; his sympathy with it in this passage is playful,
not to say ironical (Dümmler, *op. cit.,* pp. 61, 62); here, as elsewhere, the dramatist-philosopher eludes classification. See Paul

This notion that the fever of modern life sets in with the departure from the simple diet of the fruits of the earth is the basis of the *Culturgeschichte* of the geographer Dicaearchus, if we may trust Porphyry's brief summary of his *History of Greek Civilization*. Men lived in the beginning like Hesiod's Golden Race; they possessed none of the arts, not even that of tilling the soil; they subsisted on nature's food, fruits and herbs, without want and without surfeit, and therefore in a state of health, leisure, peace, and amity. There was no struggle for existence, no ground for strife, no cause for war. Then came the pastoral stage when people began to own property, to eat flesh, and to live luxuriously. Then arose envy, dissension, wars, which increased in the more elaborate life of the agricultural stage.[29]

Dicaearchus was known to Rousseau and perhaps influenced him,[30] but the exact analogue to the "Back to Nature" cult in the eighteenth century is to be found in the teaching, and apparently in the practice, of the Cynics, notably Antisthenes and Diogenes. Like Rousseau, they condemned Prometheus as the great enemy of mankind.[31] The gods had withheld fire because they desired that men should continue in the ideal state of the Golden Age. The arts and institutions of civilization have enslaved us to effeminacy,

Shorey "Plato, Lucretius, and Epicurus," *Harvard Studies in Class. Philology*, XII, 208.

[29] Müller, *Frag. Hist. Graec.*, II, 233.

[30] Pöhlmann, *Geschichte des antiken Kommunismus und Sozialismus*, I, 113.

[31] Gomperz, *op. cit.*, II, 117; Dio Chrys. *Or.* vi. 25, 30.

luxury, and injustice. Hardiness, self-sufficiency, and spontaneous kindness are to be found only in the natural state or among the lower animals.[32] For the Cynics drew lessons, not only from uncivilized people, but from the animal world; like Walt Whitman, they—

Could turn and live with animals, they are so placid and self-contained.

. . . .

They do not sweat and whine about their condition
They do not lie awake in the dark and weep for their sins.
Not one is dissatisfied, not one is demented with the mania of owning things.
Not one kneels to another nor to his kind that lived thousands of years ago.
Not one is respectable or unhappy over the whole earth.[33]

From the Cynics the doctrine is taken over by the Stoics. Zeno, the founder of the school, defined the ideal society as a state of nature where the characteristic features of the modern city are conspicuously absent: it has no temples, no gymnasiums, no law courts, no money, no slaves, no private property even in women and children,[34] and it becomes a commonplace of Stoic thought that the course of civilization has been steadily away from the natural kindness and contentment of the Golden Age. Aratus, for example, draws a pretty picture of the good old days when men had not yet sailed the sea in search of gain, but were

---
[32] Dio Chrys. *Or.* vi. 21-34.
[33] *Ibid.*, xl. 32.   [34] Diog. Laert. vii. 33.

satisfied to till the soil and to subsist on the produce of their fields. The spirit of Justice then lived on earth, ever present with men and ever heeded by them, and there was no strife, no lawsuits, no slaughter. In the less righteous Silver Age Justice retired to the mountains, whence she came down at evening to chide the people for their sins and to warn them of evils to come. When the cruel race of bronze was born, which was the first to forge the sword and slay oxen for food,[35] she withdrew altogether from this odious generation and went to dwell in the heavens.[36] Posidonius, also, the last representative of Greek Stoicism and a great popularizer of the doctrine to the Roman world, associated justice with the golden simplicity of the life of primitive man, and regarded the slaughter of animals for food as the fatal step toward organized cruelty and war.[37]

Now these thinkers were not merely playing with traditional fancies to express their revolt against the shams and shows of artificial society; neither could they have been blind to the fact that civilization represents, at least in some respects, an advance over primitive conditions; πόλις ἄνθρωπον διδάσκει (the

[35] See Plutarch's use of these lines in his sketch of the progress of cruelty from the killing of animals to the wholesale slaughter of men in war, Περὶ Σαρκοφαγίας, 998 A-B.
[36] *Phaenomena* 101-34.
[37] "primaque e caede ferarum
Incaluisse putem maculatum sanguine ferrum" [Ovid *Met*. xv. 107].

Ovid's picture of degeneration is probably derived, through Varro, from Posidonius; see Arnold, *Roman Stoicism*, p. 194, and Georges Lafaye, *Les Metamorphoses d'Ovide et leurs modèles grecs*, pp. 198-202.

state is the school of man) was a truth as obvious to them as to Simonides. They were not, however, obsessed by our modern habit of measuring progress in terms of "Twentieth Century Limiteds" and high explosives.[38] On the contrary, the ancient sages from Socrates to Marcus Aurelius emphasize the insignificance of the external trappings and circumstances of life and the all-importance of that right state of the soul in relation to other souls which they called δικαιοσύνη (justice); and the reactionary view which prevails from the fourth century on evidently rests on a sincere conviction that whatever gains civilization may have made have been won at the expense of that social sympathy and kindness which are fundamental for human well-being. Even Lucretius, who is our best source for the theory of progress, cannot shake himself free from a cynical view of contemporary civilization;[39] his doctrine of the simple life according to nature differs very little from that of the Cynics and the Stoics,[40] his picture of the life of primitive man borrows attractive colors from the Hesiodic description of the Golden Race [41] and anticipates in many points the ideal savage of Rousseau.[42] Existence had its tragedies then, such as occasional death from wild beasts, but it

---

[38] This point is sufficiently emphasized by Ferrero, *Ancient Rome and Modern America*, p. 46 and *passim*.

[39] For a full discussion of the problem presented by Lucretius' inconsistency, see Eduard Norden, "Philosophische Ansichten über die Entstehung des Menschengeschlechts, seine kulturelle Entwicklung und das goldene Zeitalter," in Fleckeisen's *Jahrbücher für Class. Phil.*, Suppl., Band 19, pp. 416 ff.

[40] See beginning of Book ii.   [41] v. 942 ff.   [42] v. 925 ff.

is left for the refined cruelty of a later age to send in
a single day thousands of men, marching with banners
spread, into the jaws of death [43]—a sentiment which
is not far removed from the Stoic commonplace that
progress in power has meant progress in cruelty
and that our inventions have been turned to our
destruction.[44]

The first influence, then, which we have to take into
account in explaining the theory of degeneration is an
out-and-out disenchantment with the results of the arts
and inventions of civilized man.[45] This alone is,
perhaps, enough to inspire poetic dreams of an ideal
past; but the well-considered doctrine of the philosophers that man in the natural state is endowed with
the fundamental social virtues, which the characteristic institutions of civilization have conspired to vitiate
or destroy, must, to some extent at least, have been
grounded on experience and observation. When they
sought for justice in the actual relations of living men,
they found it, not in the τρυφῶσα πόλις (luxurious
state), as Plato calls it, but in the more simple life
of peasants and shepherds where πλεονεξία (greed)
had not dried up the milk of human kindness; [46] and

[43] v. 988 ff.
[44] Seneca *N.Q.* 5. 18. 15, "nihil invenies tam manifestae utilitatis
quod non in contrarium transeat culpa"; cf. Tibull. i. 10. 1-6, and
Kirby Smith's commentary
[45] "Eine übersättigte Cultur, im Ekel vor sich selbst," Rohde, *op.
cit.*, p. 216.

[46] "Beatus ille qui procul negotiis,
ut prisca gens mortalium,
paterna rura bobus exercet suis,
Solutus omni faenore."

among far-away races whose primitive conditions had remained undisturbed by contact with the sophisticated world.

The ethnology of so-called primitive peoples has always presented striking contrasts to the life of civilization, and these contrasts have not always favored the latter. Professor Tylor in his chapter on the "Development of Culture," admits that "ethnographers, who seek in modern savages types of the remotely ancient human race at large, are bound by such examples to consider the rude life of primeval man under favorable conditions to have been, in its measure, a good and happy life." [47]   He refers to the experience of Sir Alfred Wallace, who says:

I have lived with communities of savages, in South America and in the East, who have no laws or law courts but the public opinion of the village freely expressed. Each man scrupulously respects the rights of his fellow, and any infriction of these rights rarely or never takes place. In such a community all are nearly equal. There are none of those wide distinctions of education and ignorance, wealth and poverty, master and servant, which are the products of our civilization; there is none of that widespread division of labor, which, while it increases wealth, also produces conflicting influences; there is not that severe competition and struggle for existence, or for wealth, which the dense population of civilized countries inevitably creates. All incitements to great crimes are thus wanting, and

[47] *Primitive Culture*, I, 30.

petty ones are repressed, partly by the influence of public opinion, but chiefly by that natural sense of justice and of his neighbor's rights, which seems to be in some degree inherent in every race of man. Now, although we have progressed vastly beyond the savage state in intellectual achievements, we have not advanced equally in morals. . . . It is not too much to say that the mass of our populations have not at all advanced beyond the savage code of morals and have in many cases sunk below it.[48]

The Greeks also had from an early period traditions of such innocent tribes, who, living simply, without differentiation of property or function, were "the justest of men." There were, for example, the Aethiopians in the extreme South and the Indians of the Far East,[49] but these were semifabulous races of whom they had no direct knowledge. Their actual experience with uncivilized tribes was drawn mainly from the contact of their settlements with the peoples north and east of the Black Sea.[50] As early as Homer we have a reference to the Mysians, who fed on the milk of mares and were "the most righteous of mankind."[51] Aeschylus in a fragment of the *Prometheus Unbound* speaks of the well-governed Scythians,

[48] *Malay Archipelago*, II, 460-61. For similar observations and generalizations, compare Stefánson, "My Quest in the Arctic," *Harper's Magazine*, CXXVI, 512; and Georg Forster's confirmation of the Garden of Eden story from his explorations with Captain Cook, cited by Myers, p. 44.

[49] Rohde, *op. cit.*, p. 218.

[50] For the experience of the Greeks with these northern tribes, see the introduction to the thorough work of Neumann, *Die Hellenen im Skythenlande.*

[51] Il. xiii. 4-6.

whose food is the milk of mares; [52] and in another
fragment of the same play [53] there is a more extended
sketch of the Gabians, a people most righteous and
kindly to strangers, who do not stir the soil with plow
or hoe, but live on the natural produce of the earth.[54]
Even Herodotus, who sees in the northern tribes
mainly unregenerate savages,[55] makes exceptions of
the Argippaeans, whose food is the fruit of trees, who
wrong no man and are wronged by none; [56] and of the
Issedonians, who, save for one savage custom, are said
to be just, and to treat their women as equals.[57]

The geographer Ephorus, who was apparently the
first to describe the Scythian tribes at any length,
contrasted two types of these northern barbarians, the
savage Ἀνθρωποφάγοι (man eaters) and a sequestered
tribe of nomads whom he identifies with Homer's
Γαλακτοφογοι (milk eaters.) The latter he describes
as dwelling in wagons, abstaining from animal food,
harming no living thing, having all things in common,
even wives and children, waging no war against
others, and free from attack because they possessed

---

[52] Nauck, 198; cf. Choerilus, frag. 13 (Didot):

μηλονόμοι δὲ Σάκαι, γενεῇ Σκύθαι . . .
νομάδων γε μὲν ἦσαν ἄποικοι
ἀνθρώπων νομίμων.

[53] Nauck, 196.

[54] It is tempting to take Eumenides, 706, οὐτ' ἐν Σκύθαισιν οὐτε Πέλοπος
ἐν τόποις to mean that Scythia and Sparta are the traditional homes
of justice, as do Riese (Die Idealisirung der Naturvölker des Nordens
in der griechischen und römischen Litteratur, p. 11) and Pöhlmann
(op. cit., I, 134), but surely the significance of these places is here
purely geographical; cf. Soph. Oed. Col., 694.

[55] iv. 127.   [56] iv. 23.   [57] iv. 26.

nothing to tempt aggression.[58] The philosopher Posidonius, whose interests embraced also geography and ethnology, devoted much attention to the Mysians, their pious scruples against taking life, their diet of milk and honey and cheese, their moral simplicity and innocence,[59] and appears to have drawn from them arguments for his theory of the original state of man in the Golden Age.[60]

There were not wanting those who, as Apollodorus, took a consistent view of savagery and dismissed such accounts as poetic moonshine.[61] Against these skeptics Strabo takes up the cudgels and challenges them to explain the fact that some of the nomad Scythians of his own day still preserved very much the same manner of life as that ascribed to them by earlier authorities, notwithstanding that by this time Greek civilization had spread its degenerative influence to almost all peoples of the world and infected them, especially where they had come into contact with the sea, with the poison of greed and inhumanity.[62]

It is easy to read both in and between the lines of Strabo's extended discussion of this question that his interest in it is not merely that of a dispassionate ethnographer, but almost that of a zealot who is defending an important article of faith.[63] His earnest-

[58] Müller, *Fr. Hist. Graec.*, I, 257, p. 257; frags. 76, 78.
[59] Strabo vii. 3. 3.
[60] Schmekel, *Die Phil. d. Mittl. Stoa.*, pp. 287-88.
[61] Πλάσματα, Strabo vii. 3. 7, 10.   [62] vii. 3. 7.
[63] vii. 3. 7, 11: ἁπλουστάτους τε γὰρ αὐτοὺς νυμίζομεν καὶ ἥκιστα κακεντρεχεῖς εὐτελεστέρους τε πολὺ ἡμῶν καὶ αὐταρκεστέρους.

ness and heat betray as evidently as if he had said it in
so many words that he is here the spokesman of a
sect who cherished the nomad Scythians as a pure
type of man in the natural state and derived from
them the principal argument for their belief in the
degenerative influence of civilization.[64]

If, furthermore, we take the outstanding features in
the description of these northern tribes—a pastoral
or prepastoral life; a frugal, mainly a vegetarian, diet;
community of property or no property at all; community of wives and children; a peaceful, orderly, and
kindly existence—and compare them with the characteristics ascribed by the philosophers to the original
state of man in the Golden Age, the correspondence is
too exact to be accidental.

But to what extent the facts suggested theory or
theory supplied the facts is, perhaps, open to discussion. The historicity of the milk-eating, peace-loving
nomads is commonly doubted; Rohde, for example,
apparently treats them as a product of the idealizing
imagination and thinks them as unreal as the
Hyperboreans; [65] and our own view is likely to be

---

[64] ἃ δοκεῖ μὲν εἰς ἡμερότητα συντείνειν διαφθείρει δὲ τὰ ἤθη καὶ ποικιλίαν
ἀντὶ τῆς ἁπλότητος . . εἰσάγει (vii. 3. 7, 22) reveals the Stoic.

[65] *Der griech. Roman,* p. 217. Rohde follows Riese, who contends
that the tradition of the nomad Scythians begins with Homer, whose
fancy sketched the first outline of a milk-eating, just-dealing, northern race, and that henceforth the Greek imagination filled in the
sketch with various ideals, mainly Pythagorean and Platonic (*op.
cit.,* pp. 20, 21). Riese dismisses the researches of Ephorus as book-
ish and second-hand. Neumann, however, regards Ephorus as a
trustworthy authority, who may idealize the customs of the Scythians, but always does so on a basis of fact (*op. cit.,* I, 315 ff.).
The crux of the problem is the community of wives and children.

determined by a more or less a priori assumption of how the Stone Man and his later representatives should have behaved in order not to disturb a con-. sistent plan of evolution. But we can at any rate be sure of these points: that the nomad Scythians of Ephorus were regarded by the Greeks generally as historical; [66] that the preponderance of ancient au-

This according to Riese is read into the institutions of the Scythians from Plato. But, in the first place, the limited communism of Plato is not the communism attributed to the Scythians; and, in the next place, Plato cannot be held responsible for the sexual promiscuity, more or less idealized, ascribed by Herodotus to the Auseans (iv. 180); to the Agathyrsians (iv. 104); and to the Massagetae (i. 216). Furthermore, it is quite clear from the last reference that the common Greek view, from which Herodotus here dissents, attributed this custom to the Scythians as did Ephorus and later writers generally (see, for ex., Nicolaus Damascenus, 123; Müller, III, 460). Indeed, such contrasts to their own marriage customs the Greeks found in many parts of the world; other examples are reported by Aristotle, *Pol.* 1262 A 19; Xanthus, frag. 28; Theopompus, frag. 222; Nicolaus, frags. 111, 135, in Müller, *Frag. Hist. Graec.;* and Diodorus ii. 58—enough to give plausibility to the dramatic exaggeration in Eur. *Andromache,* 173 ff:

τοιοῦτον πᾶν τὸ βάρβαρον γένος
πατήρ τε θυγατρὶ παῖς τε μητρὶ μίγνυται
κόρη τ᾽ ἀδελφῷ. . : . . .
. . . . καὶ τῶν δ᾽ οὐδὲν ἐξείργει νόμος.

For parallels from modern ethnology, see Andrew Lang's article "Family," in *Encyclopaedia Britannica.*

No one denies, so far as I know, that the customs of the so-called nature peoples have been "idealized" in interpretation, as when Strabo says that the Scythians had wives and children in common πλατονικῶς (vii. 3. 7) or when Lewis Morgan finds the exact conditions of his "Maylayan" or "Consanguine" family in Plato's *Timaeus* 18 C, D. (*Ancient Society,* p. 417); but it seems more probable that ethnological facts, however imperfectly understood, should have given suggestion to theory (see Gomperz, II, 413; Barker, *op. cit.,* p. 152; Dümmler, *op. cit.,* p. 56; and Adam's edition of Plato's *Republic,* I, 355) than that Plato's ideal of communism should have been foisted on the nomad Scythians and other primitive peoples.

[66] Strabo vii. 3. 7, 10. αὕτη ἡ ὑπόληψις καὶ νῦν ἔτι συμμένει παρὰ τοῖς Ἕλλησιν.

thority is in favor of this view; and that there is ethnologically no improbability in attributing to un-civilized tribes of that time the unspoiled simplicity and the substantial virtues which Stefánson found in the Eskimos who had never seen a white man, and which led him to infer that "the hand of evolution had written the Golden Rule in the hearts of the contem-poraries of the mammoth millenniums before the Pyramids were built." [67]

We are, then, in accord with the testimony of an-tiquity as well as with modern experience in conclud-ing that the Greeks in their contact with uncivilized peoples found two sets of facts—one which supported the view that primeval man existed in a slough of brutish savagery, the other that he lived in an Eden of innocent simplicity; that at the time of exultant pride in their own life and contempt for what lay outside of it they seized on savage and revolting prac-tices among the wild barbarians as typical of the dark age from which they were confidently pressing for-ward to a golden future; and that later in a period of discontent and disillusionment their philosophers em-phasized the uncorrupted virtues of primitive races to prove that time must "run back and fetch the Age of Gold." [68]

[67] "My Quest in the Arctic," *Harper's Magazine,* CXXVI, 512.
[68] The poetic fancy of Milton and Virgil and Shelley that the Golden Age will be restored is also a Stoic hope. See Kirby Smith's article "Ages of the World" in *Hastings' Encyclopaedia of Religion and Ethics,* I, 198.

AN ODIOUS COMPARISON [1]

Some time ago I found myself in a Los Angeles hotel without any money. I had, however, a small New York draft which I presented confidently at the desk. I say confidently, for I had been struck, as has every traveler in California, by the accommodating eagerness of the people of that State to honor drafts, checks, or any other such evidence of a disposition to part with one's possessions. Imagine, therefore, my chagrin when the clerk demanded, in that supercilious tone which I suppose the privileged have taken with suppliants since the beginning of time, whether I had any one who could identify me. I said, "No, I am an utter stranger here." Now ordinarily being a stranger in Los Angeles is a sufficient guarantee of respectability, but my identity as a tourist was, it seems, in question. The clerk retired and presently returned with the manager. Again I was chilled by a cold scrutiny; again I was hurt by searching questions. Had I no way of proving that I was sailing under my own colors—no letters, no credentials of any kind? I searched through the pockets of my coat, in vain; of my vest, in vain. I began to grow suspicious of myself when my fingers in their nervous excursions to

[1] Phi Beta Kappa address, University of Missouri, June, 1917.

69

and fro chanced upon my watch fob and my golden key. I seized upon it with joyous relief. "Here," I said, "is the token of my membership in Phi Beta Kappa. You see my name inscribed upon it and the place and time of my election." He looked at it gingerly, almost shrinking as from something weird and uncanny; and finally, as if eager to get back on mortal and familiar ground, he asked "You haven't got an Elk's card about your clothes, have you?"

Ladies and gentlemen, it was a trying situation on which I do not care to dwell. I will only say that I tried then as I have tried since to show myself worthy of our traditions. I summoned what I could of academic dignity; I tried hard to be "the captain of my soul." But it was difficult then and I confess I have often found it difficult since. Will you forgive me if I say that I find it difficult now? I think I know what a Phi Beta Kappa address ought to be; I think I know that it is expected to drop gently upon the ears from the heights of an unruffled, Olympian calm. "It is sweet," said the placid philosopher, "to look upon the mighty contests of war arrayed along the plains without yourself sharing in the danger; it is sweet to hold the lofty and serene positions well fortified by the learning of the wise from which you may look down upon others and see them wandering all abroad and going astray in their search for the path of life, . . . their striving night and day with surpassing effort to struggle up to the summit of power and be masters of the world."

I, however, cannot rise to such philosophical aloofness. I am of the world in which men appear to have
dethroned Zeus and set up the idol Whirligig, and I
reel with the common vertigo. I am of the world in
which men pluck the God of Nations by the ear and
chat familiarly with *"unserem guten alten deutschen
Gott dort oben,"* and I find myself dazed and bewil-
dered with the rest. I am of the world which has observed with admiration, not to say affection, the rise
of a wonderful people to imperial greatness, to a first
place in commerce, in beneficent social legislation, in
effective political organization, in the councils of the
nations, in science, in literature, in the arts—a people
so rich in what we term the gifts of civilization that
their wealth has overflowed their boundaries and penetrated all the world—a people who have given us many
of our best Americans—a people who have taught many
of us in their universities and impressed us by their
kindness, their sentiment, even their softness of heart;
and I am of the world which has seen that people turn
to the worship of iron, *"Gott der Eisen wachsen liess,"*
preach the gospel of hate, exalt cruelty to a virtue, and
justify itself as the cyclone or the flood might justify
itself, by the necessity of its own existence.

It seems a contradiction in nature, a reversal of the
inevitable order of things. It is as if a tree should
grow downward, or the sun fall from the sky, or the
stars crash about our heads. It is Nietzsche's "transvaluation of all values" with a vengeance. I can think
of nothing else; I can speak of nothing else. The most

that I can do is to view it not as a thing altogether unique, not as some new diabolism hoarded up by malicious Fate against our time, but as an old tragedy on a new stage, and, seeing it in this light, to derive for myself such mental comfort as comes from stripping away the vague terrors of the unknown.

Some twenty-four centuries ago the greatest of Greek historians told the grim story of the Peloponnesian War. He characterized that protracted struggle as the most terrible within the memory of man. It engaged practically the whole of what was then the significant world; all the Greek states were involved sooner or later, and barbarians as well. It was a world war and a world calamity. Famine and plague conspired with slaughter and exile to debase the spirit of man. Never had there been such a complete "transvaluation of all values." "Words," says Thucydides, "had no longer the same relation to things. Reckless aggression was loyal courage; prudential delay was the excuse of a coward; frantic energy was the true quality of a man; the lover of violence alone was free from the charge of hypocrisy; the seal of good faith was not divine law but fellowship in crime; the honest simplicity which is so large a part of a noble nature was laughed to scorn and disappeared. Striving in every way to overcome each other, men committed the most monstrous crimes, observing neither the bounds of justice nor of expediency, but making the caprice of the moment their law. Those who were of neither party fell a prey to both; either they were disliked because they held aloof or men were jealous of their surviving. Human nature, having trampled under foot all laws, delighted to show that her passions were ungovernable, that she was stronger than justice, and the enemy of everything above her. . . . But when men are retaliating upcn others they are reckless of the future and do not hesitate to annul those common laws of humanity to which every individual trusts for his hope of deliverance should he ever be overtaken by calamity. They forget that in their own hour of need they will look for them in vain." [2]

Such are some of the dark colors in which the Athenian historian draws the picture of events which occurred in his own time "and of like events," he adds with gloomy clairvoyance, "which may be expected to happen hereafter in the order of human things."

I am aware that the distinguished President Emeritus of Harvard University has recently warned us against taking our instruction from ancient history. "The social and individual problems of life were," he objects, "simpler in the ancient world than in the modern, and they were often solved by giving play to the elemental passions of human nature; so that the study of them affords but imperfect guidance to wise action amid the wider and more complex conditions of the modern world." It would be presumption on my part not to respect the words of so wise a

---

[2] The renderings from Thucydides are, for the most part, those of Jowett.

man and so ripe a scholar, and it is with diffidence that I venture the opinion that the distinction between ancient and modern times is not that human nature was more elemental then than now. It was undoubtedly more simple, more frank, more itself, more naked than now. Modern civilization is more millineristic, more artificially, more fantastically dressed. Our motives, our impulses, our aspirations even are more elaborately be-wigged, be-rouged and be-high-heeled; and when we approach the ancients with our passion for disguises, we are apt to be shocked, as Dr. Eliot is shocked, to find them insufficiently clothed.

If this is a real difference, and I believe it is, it may be questioned whether it is the part of a sound education to shun altogether the ancient simplicities and directnesses for the more impenetrable proprieties and complexities of a later world. In any case we must take our parallels where we find them, and I can find no such illuminating parallel to the outstanding features of the present cataclysm as is found in Thucydides' account of the Peloponnesian War and particularly of the tragic career of Athens in the course of that war. The parallel has been noted more than once. Gilbert Murray has touched upon it in the preface to his translation of the *Trojan Woman* of Euripides; Irving Babbitt has mentioned it in a clever article in *The Nation;* and all students of Greek history must in these last years have read into the empty saying that history repeats itself a fulness of ominous verity.

That ancient world war, like all wars that have ever

happened, had its roots in the past. In order to appre-
ciate anything of its significance we must go back fifty
years to the conflict between the Greeks and the Persians, which, I need not remind you, was essentially a
struggle between Eastern despotism and free institutions. Again and again the pages of Herodotus, the
historian of this war, are lighted up by the Hellenic
worship of liberty, of the right of each state to work
out its own salvation in its own way, to be free to
make and obey its own commands. Freedom was as
yet a new and glorious birth in the world, and never
before or since has it seemed so sweet as then when it
confronted its first terrible danger. "Tyranny,"
Herodotus makes one of his characters say, "Tyranny,"
disturbs ancient laws, violates women and kills men
without trial; but a free people ruling themselves have
in the first place the most beautiful name in the world,
and in the next place, they do none of these things."
I need not remind you either that in this fight of the
Greeks for freedom Athens among the Greek states
played the noblest part. Sinking her own ambitions
in a common cause, yielding to others the precedence
she herself deserved, thinking first of Hellas and second
of herself, she proved herself, as Herodotus says in
his matter of fact way, the "Savior of the Greeks."

And she had her reward. Many, a great many, of
the Greek states forgot for the time being their local
pride and jealousy and enrolled themselves right will-
ingly under her leadership in a league to make the
world safe against tyranny. The records of the years

from the formation of this so-called Confederacy of Delos to the outbreak of the Peloponnesian War are sadly incomplete, but even so they reveal a steady outflow of energy from Athens which is astounding. Consider her military exploits alone, and you would think that she had no time for anything but fighting. Consider how active she was in erecting fortifications and in beautifying the city, and the Acropolis, and you would think that she had no time for anything but building. Consider her political history, the rapid steps by which her government at home became a true partnership of all the citizens in the high business of the state, and you would think that she must have concentrated on political reform. Consider her achievements in letters, and you would think that her vitality must have been chiefly of the spirit. Consider that while she was doing all this and more, she was busy welding the restless, centrifugal units of the confederacy into an empire, and you throw up your hands and exclaim with Pindar: δαιμόνιον πτολίεθρον, a city of more-than-men!

Is it any wonder, human nature being what it has been till now, that with this energy Athens grew ambitious to energize the world? Is it any wonder that she sought to extend the sphere of her beneficent influence? Is it any wonder that she said to the members of her empire when they grew weary of basking in her glory, "You are better off with us," and accompanied the words by an invincible gesture of power? Is it any wonder that, knowing by intuition and experience that her institutions were the best in the world, she should have sent them abroad with her armies and ships of war and forced them upon those who preferred their own? And is it any wonder, human nature being what it has been till now, that Athens, once best beloved of Greek states as champion of liberty, came to be execrated by most of the world as a tyrant?

When Herodotus called Athens the "Savior of Greece," the Peloponnesian War had already begun, and he felt it necessary to preface his eulogy with these words: "Here I am compelled by the facts to express an opinion which will be offensive to most of mankind." And Thucydides makes the hatred against Athens still clearer: "The feeling of mankind was strongly on the side of the Spartans, for they were now the avowed liberators of Hellas. Cities and individuals were eager to assist them to the utmost both by word and deed. In general the indignation against the Athenians was intense; some were trying to be delivered from them and others fearful of falling under their sway."

This, then, is the situation of Athens at the beginning of the War: the strongest military power in Greece at the head of an empire now held together by force; isolated by the fear and hostility of the rest of the world and on the whole proud of that isolation, for, in a sense, it was the isolation of greatness. "Consider," says one of the Corinthian envoys, speaking to the Spartans, "what manner of men are these Athe-

nians with whom you will have to fight. They are bold
beyond their strength; they run risks which prudence
would condemn; but in the midst of misfortunes they
are full of hope. When conquerors they pursue their
victory to the utmost; when defeated they fall back
the least. Their bodies they devote to their country
as though they belonged to other men; their true self
is their mind which is most truly their own when employed in her service. When they do not carry out an
intention which they have formed they seem to themselves to have sustained a personal bereavement; when
an enterprise succeeds, they have gained a mere instal-
ment of what is to come, but if they fail they at once
conceive new hopes and so fill up the void. With them
alone, to hope is to have, for they lose not a moment
in the execution of an idea. This is the lifelong task,
full of danger and toil, which they are always imposing
on themselves. To do their duty is their only holiday
and they deem the quiet of inaction to be as disagree-
able as the most tiresome business. If a man should
say of them in a word that they were born neither to
have peace themselves nor allow peace to other men,
he would simply speak the truth."

These are words which Thucydides puts into the
mouth of an enemy. What a great Athenian could say
on the same subject he records in the splendid funeral
oration spoken by Pericles in honor of his countrymen
who fell in the first battles of the War:

"To sum up—I say that Athens is the school of
Hellas and that the individual Athenian in his own

person seems to have the power of adapting himself to the most varied forms of action with the utmost versatility and grace. This is no passing and idle word but truth and fact; and the assertion is verified by the position to which these qualities have raised the state. For in the hour of trial Athens alone among her contemporaries is superior to the report of her. No enemy who comes against her is indignant at the reverses which he sustains at the hands of such a city; no subject complains that his masters are unworthy of him. And we shall assuredly be not without witnesses; there are mighty monuments of our power which will make us the wonder of this and succeeding ages; we shall not need the praises of Homer or of any other panegyrist whose poetry may please for the moment . . . For we have compelled every land and every sea to open a path to our valor and have everywhere planted memorials of our friendship and our enmity. Such is the city for whose sake these men nobly fought and died; they could not bear the thought that she might be taken from them; and everyone of us who survive should gladly toil in her behalf."

I have taken but a paragraph from a wonderful eulogy of a wonderful people. If there breathes through it a feeling that this sacred city is so lifted above the levels of ordinary humanity as to be "beyond good and evil," that it is the sanctuary of civilization, the leaven which is to leaven the world; if, in a word, the speech of Pericles has a taint of *hubris* in it, this is at least as easy for us to excuse, as it is for

Kuno Francke, in his apology for Germany, to justify "that spirit of superciliousness, which, as a very natural concomitant of a century of extraordinary achievement, has developed, especially during the last twenty-five years, in the ruling classes of Germany." There is such a thing as pardonable pride in accomplishments which promise well for humanity. Compare the words of a less restrained spokesman for German ideals: "The world dominion of which Germany dreams is not blind to the lessons of the Napoleonic tyranny. Force alone, violence or brute strength by its mere presence or by its loud manifestation in war, may be necessary to establish this dominion, but its ends are spiritual. The triumph of the empire will be the triumph of German *Kultur,* of the German world vision in all its phases and departments of human life and energy; in religion, in poetry, in science, arts, politics, and in social endeavor." The utterance of Pericles is infinitely higher in tone, but its essence is the same. Power is not an end in itself. *Faust-recht* rests upon *Kultur-recht.* The will to dominate is sublimated by the crusader's zeal.

But listen again to Pericles when the reverses and rancors of war have touched even that great soul with cynicism: "Do not imagine that you are fighting about a simple issue, freedom or slavery. You have an empire to lose and there is the danger to which your imperial rule has exposed you. Neither can you resign your power if at this crisis any timorous or inactive spirit is for playing the honest man. For by this time your empire has become a tyranny which in the opinion of mankind may have been unjustly gained but cannot be safely surrendered. These men (i. e., men whom scruples of justice rob of power of aggression) would soon ruin a city, and if they were to go and found a state of their own they would equally ruin that."

When Pericles said this he was a sick and discouraged man, and had not long to live. Even so, the brutal implication of his statement is redeemed by the dignity of a nature which could never be ignoble. It remained for a blatant successor to his leadership of the war party in Athens to speak more frankly. Pleading before the Athenian Assembly for a policy of frightfulness Cleon shouted: "Do not be misled by the most deadly enemies of empire, pity and fine words and equity"—a sentiment upon which the mad philosopher of modern Germany has set the seal of his high approval. "In vigorous eras," says Nietzsche, "noble civilizations see something contemptible in sympathy, in brotherly love, in lack of self-assertion and self-reliance."

Long before this time, the poet Hesiod had laid down the principle which was good enough for old-fashioned Greece: "For the birds of the air and the beasts of the field hath Zeus ordained one law: that they prey upon one another; but for man hath he ordained justice which is by far the best." But a new philosophy was now changing all that. There is but one law: The big eat the little, the mighty inherit the earth. Moral commands and prohibitions—pity, mercy, brotherly love, good faith, just dealing—are mere conventions, mere conspiracies entered into by the weak against the strong, and have no justification whatever in the nature of things. Might is the only right. "Nature herself," says a speaker in Plato's *Gorgias*, "proves that it is right for the better man to exploit the worse, for the stronger to exploit the weaker. Again and again she reveals this truth both in the case of the animals and in the case of men in states and nations. By what right did Xerxes lead his army against Greece, or Darius march against the Scythians? One could give countless instances in which people act according to the law of nature, and not according to that artificial law which we set up when we attempt to mold the best and strongest among us, taking them in hand when they are young, taming, as it were, our lion-cubs with magic formulas and spells, and try to make slaves out of them by preaching that we should enjoy equality and that this is beautiful and right. But in spite of us, when a man is born with a nature strong enough, he shakes himself free of all these shackles, smashes through our hedges, tramples under foot our scraps of paper, our hypocritical tricks and charms and laws which are against nature; and lo! our slave stands over us revealed as our master, and the justice of nature dawns in splendor."

Such doctrines were in the air, and lent no little aid and comfort to the rampant chauvinism of the period.

They stand out naked and unashamed in the plea by which the Athenians justified the atrocity of Melos. The little Island of Melos had steadily refused to take sides in the war and for a season was left in peace. Her neutrality was, however, a moral challenge to the Athenian Empire, and at the opportune time the Athenians landed a force upon Melos and demanded the submission of her people. Thucydides devotes page after page to the negotiations which were carried on, and the speeches which he records on both sides present very vividly a dramatic conflict of national aspirations moving grimly to its tragic climax. The Athenian actors drop all disguise of fine words. The Melians, they admit, had never harmed them; their only offense was their defenselessness, and they must yield to the empire of the strong. No Treitschke had as yet uttered the famous dictum that "Among all political sins, the sin of feebleness is the most contemptible; it is the political sin against the Holy Ghost." But such was substantially the Athenian argument. The Melians, in their turn, urge that it is their right to be free, that justice is on their side, and that therefore they are confident of the favor of Heaven—to which the Athenians reply:

"As for the gods, we expect to have quite as much of their favor as you, for we are not doing or claiming anything which goes beyond common opinion concerning divine or men's desires about human things. For of the gods we believe and of men we know that by a law of their nature wherever they can rule they will.

This law was not made by us and we are not the first to have acted upon it and shall bequeath it to all time, and we know that you and all mankind, if you were as strong as we, would do as we do. . . . Surely you cannot dream of flying to that false sense of honor which has been the ruin of so many when danger stared them in the face. Many men with their eyes still open to the consequences have found the word "honor" too much for them and have suffered a mere name to lure them on until it has drawn down upon them real and irretrievable calamities; through their own folly they have incurred a worse dishonor than fortune would have inflicted upon them. If you are wise, you will not run this risk. You ought to see that there can be no disgrace in yielding to a great city which invites you to become her ally on reasonable terms, keeping your own land and merely paying tribute, and you will certainly gain no honor, if, having to choose between two alternatives, safety and war, you obstinately prefer the worse."

Incredibly and nobly the Melians preferred "honor" and "the worse." "Men of Athens," they said, "our resolution is unchanged and we will not in a moment surrender the liberty which our city, founded seven hundred years ago, still enjoys. We will trust to the good fortune which by the favor of the gods has hitherto preserved us . . . and endeavor to save ourselves." Vain hope and trust! God was on the side of the strongest battalions; and "the Athenians," says Thucydides, speaking with restrained and unnatural calm, "put to death all the Melians who were of military age and made slaves of the women and children."

It may be that in some unearthly Island of the Blest the Melian dead are justified of their faith, but not in the world we know.

O thou Pomegranate of the Sea
Sweet Melian Isle across the years
   Thy Belgian sister calls to thee
In anguished sweat of blood and tears.

Her fate like thine—a ruthless band
Hath ravaged all her loveliness.
   How Athens spoiled thy prosperous land
Athenian lips with shame confess.

Thou too a land of lovely arts
Of potter's and of sculptor's skill.
   Thy folk of high undaunted hearts
As those that throb in Belgium still.

Within thy harbor's circling rim
The warships long with banners bright
   Sailed bearing Athens' message grim
'God hates the weak, Respect our Might.'

The flames within thy fanes grew cold
Stilled by the foeman's swarming hords,
   Thy sons were slain, thy daughters sold
To serve the lusts of stranger lords.

For Attic might thou didst defy,
Thy folks the foeman slew as sheep,

Across the years hear Belgium's cry,
'O sister of the wine-dark deep,

'Whose cliffs gleam seaward roseate,
Not one of all thy martyr roll
But keeps his faith inviolate;
Man kills our body, not our soul.' [3]

Thucydides has given us something more than an accurate chronicle of events. He has given us a great picture of the soul of Athens, of the breaking down of moral standards, of time-honored ideals, by lust for power reinforced by rancor and hate. He has given us a drama of the fall of man. Evidently he regards the Melian episode as the tragic climax. The real catastrophe is not Athens, once an imperial city, later moaning amid the ruins of her glory, but Athens once the savior of Greece for freedom now saying to Melos, "It is a crime not to be a slave."

"Whom the gods would destroy they first make mad." After Melos, Thucydides represents the Athenians as seized by an infatuate recklessness. Throwing aside henceforth all pretense of military necessity, they embarked on that disastrous robber expedition to Sicily whose frank purpose was the conquest and plunder of the rich settlements of what was then the Western World.

Absit omen. I do not desire to press the parallel in all its details. I do not desire to overemphasize the itch for world-dominion in Germany which may in-

[3] The lines are by Grace Harriet MacCurdy.

clude designs upon our own resources. "Comparisons
are odious." Lovers of Athens will think that I have
strained the parallel; admirers of Germany will not
concede its significance. There are of course as many
points of contrast as of resemblance. But on this
ancient stage the Treitschkes, the Bernhardis, the
Nietzsches, the Bethmann-Hollwegs, the scraps of
paper—all the nightmare shapes of military necessity
—play their sinister parts. The form changes, the
spirit remains.

I do not mean to say that Athens alone in her time
and that Germany alone in her time have run amuck
in this way. Megalomania is not a rare disease. To
the Greek mind it is a sort of original sin. It battens
on prosperity; it is held in check only by the buffets
of adversity. Unusual achievement, extraordinary
power, breed that full-blown domineering pride which
they called *hubris; hubris* breeds the tyrant; and history in its largest aspects is a process of knocking bul-
lies in the head. Perhaps this is too simple, and will
not do for our modern complexities. But surely it has
its measure of truth. That golden balance of modesty
and self-respect, which the Greeks named *sophrosuné*
is still the supremely important virtue for men and
nations, and there will be no living together in peace
until we have it in a greater degree.

The war has already chastened us all. I hardly
recognize my fellow-countrymen; the spirit of brag is
so strangely absent. Let us hope, let us pray, that it
is the modesty of a giant gathering all his mighty

strength against a powerful enemy. Even Germany has come to see that there are laws beyond her fancied necessities; perhaps Maximilian Harden is right; perhaps she has even now "learned the mysterious ways of Providence." To bring that lesson home is the object of this war. Whatever dark currents may once have coursed beneath this mad upheaval, the issue is now splendidly clear. We now know what we are fighting for; we are fighting and must fight to a finish for *sophrosuné;* we are fighting for the spirit of *live and let live.* And to that spirit there must be no exception; no *vae victis* has ever saved the world, nor ever will. The dying words of Edith Cavell have pronounced the sweet evangel which should melt even the rigor of the system which destroyed her: "Standing as I do in view of God and Eternity, I realize that patriotism is not enough. I must have no hatred or bitterness toward anyone."

LIBERATING HIGHER EDUCATION

There are some who still quote with approval Matthew Arnold's tribute to Sophocles as one "who saw life steadily and saw it whole," notwithstanding that in our generation this counsel to perfection is in danger of becoming a mere intellectual curiosity.

It was easier to see life steadily in ancient Athens— that city of reposeful beauty set like a jewel between the mountains and the sea—in an age long before the machinery of rapid transit had imbued men with a passion to be restlessly on the go from one group of smoking chimneys to another.

It is harder to see life steadily in this age of movies, Fords, tramweys, subways, elevateds, and limiteds, when the latest word of our mechanistic philosophy appropriately defines existence as a "discontinuous series of jerks with nothing between."

But if it is harder for us to see life steadily, it is even more difficult to see it whole. Here again Sophocles had the advantage over us. It was easier to see life whole when the cosmos was limited to a little patch of earth and sea and sky, before navigation and exploration had penetrated every nook and corner of our globe, before the telescope had disclosed an infinity of worlds beyond worlds, and before the

89

microscope and the delicate devices of our science laboratories had revealed an infinity of worlds within worlds.

It was easier to see life whole when the body of learning was as yet readily grasped by a single mind, before the centuries had accumulated that tremendous mass of ill-assorted knowledge which now baffles our powers of integration.

It was easier to see life whole when men knew no other than the simple life; when philosophers could preach, unmolested, upon the streets the now amazing doctrine that the richest man is not he who has the greatest number of possessions, but who has the fewest wants; before modern industrialism had exalted acquisitiveness to a supreme place among the virtues, and before the alluring advertisements of every commodity under the sun and the compelling salesmanship of modern commerce had created a race of human beings who are bewildering complexes of jaded or unsatisfied desires.

It was easier to see life whole when human relations were warm and personal and so productive of that sympathy which cements men together in a co-operative commonwealth, before coal and iron and steam and electricity had mechanized society, before modern miracles of rapid communication and transit had made the world one great neighborhood without neighborliness, and before industrial organization on a giant scale had brought about that geographical and sentimental divorce between classes—between, for ex-

ample, employers and employed—which threatens the
very disruption of our social order.

Happy Sophocles in his simple world and limited
horizon! Yet the man in the street to-day would not
trade places with him; he would look down with pity
upon the barbarism of an age unblessed by telephones,
phonographs, electric lights and motor cars. He would
be amused if he could hear the ode in which Sophocles
glorified the progress of man:

> There are marvellous wonders many
> Where'er this world we scan,
> Yet among them nowhere any
> So great a marvel as Man.
> To the white sea's uttermost verges
> Afloat this miracle goes,
> Forging through thundering surges
> When the wintry southwind blows:
>
>   *   *   *
>
> The blithe swift careless races
> On light wing flying in air
> With speed of his wit he chases
> And takes in a woven snare:
> All deer in the wildwood running,
> The deep sea's diverse kind,
> Are snared in toils by the cunning
> Of Man's outrivaling mind.
> Strength of the lion, lord of the hill,
> Yields to Man's overmastering skill;
> With his proud mane bowing under the yoke
> The rebellious horse is tamed and broke,

And the mountain bull to his will.
He hath found out speech, and the giving
Of wings to his high proud Thought:
And the ordered spirit of living
In towns his mind hath taught;
Shelter from arrowy shafts
Of the bleak air's frost and sleet;
There is nought in store but his crafts
Shall have armed him ready to meet;
He fronts with fresh devices
The future's every shape:
Only, despite his cunning,
The Grave still mocks all shunning;
Disease may root her vices,
But Art hath learned escape.[1]

The man in the street would smile at such achievements as mere child's play. What were the little triremes of that age, propelled by hand precariously over an inland sea, compared to our dreadnoughts and ocean greyhounds? What did the invention of speech amount to in an age which could not "listen in" to the babble and the jabber of a continent? How trifling seems the subjection of the beasts to us, who have subdued the very elements to our will, who plunge into depths of the sea where no fish could follow, who soar to heights of the air where no eagle would dare climb. In fine, how like pygmies appear the men of that day beside our supermen! We have science, we have knowledge, we have power—or we think we have. We

[1] Translation by Walter Headlam.

press a button and darkness is turned into day; we push a lever and go hurtling through space. And we pity Sophocles who could do none of these things.

Yet in fact we understand but little the collective power and progress of our day. We forget that if we were cast away upon a desert shore, or upon some *Erewhon* whence modern inventions had been banished, we should be more helpless, more at the mercy of a primitive environment than the rudest savage; so little are we the masters, so much are we the slaves of our inventions. We forget that if we could recall Sophocles from the shades into the world in which we live, while he would at first be utterly amazed by the infinite machinery of modern life, he would soon be pressing the same buttons and pushing the same levers and be quite as civilized as we.

The great difference between the contemporaries of Sophocles and ourselves lies not in any improvement of mentality. It would be a rash man, it would certainly be an ignorant man, who would claim for us a superior intelligence, a superior wisdom, or even a superior general knowledge. The difference lies in the fact that there has been stored up for us by scholars and scientists from generation to generation an immense reservoir of knowledge. Someone taps this reservoir at one point and we have the steam engine; someone taps it at another point and gives us the dynamo; someone in like manner gives the gas engine or the airplane or the radiograph. And so invention is added to invention, mechanism to mechanism, wheel to wheel, wire to wire, power to power, motion to motion, friction to friction, noise to noise, until we have, whether for good or for ill, that vast and intricate machine, that appalling complex which we call our industrial civilization.

To live in the thick of this confused complexity is not, as many seem to think, in itself a liberal education. There is, no doubt, a kind of stimulation in the multiplication of the superficial contacts of life, a quickening of the nerves, an increase in alertness—as of one who must pick and dodge his precarious way amid the traffic of a modern city. But what of the mental poise, what of the broad outlook, what of the understanding, what of the wisdom to control and use to good purpose the accelerating speed, the growing power, the increasing wealth of our time? Surely the most swaggering optimist, seeing the world moving daily in the direction of greater complexity, of vaster organization, and of more minute specialization of function, can hardly escape some feeling of misgiving as he becomes aware of the increasing power of the industrial revolution to reduce human life to machinery, to make us mere bolts or cogs or rivets, to condemn us to see life in fragments and live it in fragments, with no comprehension of the whole, with no integrating vision to give meaning and zest to our isolated tasks.

> For most men in a brazen prison live,
> Where in the sun's hot eye
> With heads bent o'er their toil, they languidly

Their lives to some unmeaning task-work give,
Dreaming of nought beyond their prison wall.

Every gain of civilization has been purchased at a price. There was a wholeness of life in primitive society, when a man found his own food, made his own clothing, and built his own shelter, which is forever gone. Now it takes a village of men to make a Ford car. It takes a hundred men to make a Douglas shoe; it takes fifty men to make a cake of Ivory Soap; it takes more than fifty of us to make a college graduate, and even then, so unrelated are the fragments of which he is composed, we cannot guarantee that he will float.

The universities have themselves been caught up in the coil of the machine; yielding to the pressure of the times, they have unwittingly aided and abetted the disintegration, the fragmentation of human life; they have turned out specialists with narrow interests; they have turned out mechanicians and technicians without vision; they have turned out bolts and cogs and rivets for the machine; they have in some degree succumbed to the popular demand and become places of apprenticeship for jobs; they have in many cases become, as the president of the largest university in America so eloquently complained a few months ago, places where men and women may learn a hundred ways of making a living without being required to share in any common or fundamental body of knowledge which might make living together itself a thing to be desired.

This condition is no longer due to any lack of agreement in our colleges and universities as to what it is desirable that everyone should know. There has been no little controversy over this question; and for some time we were so much confused and perplexed amid the bellicose claims of rival departments of knowledge that we were content to leave the choice mainly to the wisdom of freshmen. But such quarrels as, for example, that between the humanists and the scientists, have been in a large measure composed, and at the present time few would dispute the view that a liberal education should give us a reliable introduction to the twofold world in which we have to live—our human world and the physical universe. But, in fact, the student in our colleges finds it hardly possible to get a liberal education in that sense of the term. Even if he were free—and wise in his freedom—to pick and choose throughout the conventional four-year course, he could not obtain such a survey of the realm of science as is presented, for instance, in the four volumes of Professor Thompson's fascinating *Outline of Science,* or such a comprehensive view of human events as Mr. Wells gives us in his much abused, but much read, history of the ages. Instead he finds the salient and significant facts of human experience and of scientific achievement filed away under manifold rubrics of "sophies," "nomies," "ologies," and "graphies," more or less fragmentarily treated in isolated "departments"—each department conducted by specialists whose interest and effort, in effect if not in intention, are centered on the training of specialists; and only incidentally in some extra-departmental "orientation" course is the attempt consciously made to educate men and women to approach the universal experiences of life with any degree of scientific vision or philosophical outlook. The introduction of such orientation courses in our universities is itself a confession that the liberal college, whose purpose is wholly that of orientation, has been allowed to drift far from its purpose.

But if the college of liberal arts in our universities is from this point of view an anomaly, having become in practice a congeries of departments each intent largely upon its own end, and not an organization for envisaging life as a whole, it should not be too roundly condemned. At any rate, the situation is explicable. The enormous increase in the sum of human knowledge, together with attempts to popularize and even to sensationalize new discoveries through nonacademic agencies, has been attended by a vast amount of loose talking, of hasty generalization and of quack philosophy—instances of the little learning which is a dangerous thing; and what is going on in our universities represents a reaction against superficiality, dilettantism and charlatanism in education. Our scholars, distrustful of the larger views and broad generalizations which agitate humanity, withdraw themselves into their laboratories to their exact measurements and tests; content to extend by ever so little the bounds of recondite knowledge; careful, oh so careful of the opinions of their fellow-savants, but careless of mankind; speaking an esoteric dialect unintelligible save to the initiated; in effect, to borrow a phrase from Professor Robinson's interesting book, "dehumanizing knowledge," and leaving the popularization of it to— the Sunday supplement.

If this is over-stating the case, yet no one can deny that there is a case, and that this state of affairs cannot safely continue in a democratic society which staggers under the terrific strains and complexities of this day. The great gulf between sound learning and the popular mind—nay, even the student mind—is a perilous thing. If people do not get true information they are bound to act upon misinformation. The conflict now raging between "fundamentalism" and "evolution" could not conceivably exist in a country so richly dotted with institutions of learning as our own if the average college student were brought into contact with the indisputable facts of our religious and of our biological inheritance.

We who sit secure in our citadels of learning are apt to view this conflict with philosophical calm, perhaps even with complacent amusement. "Nothing is more pleasant," said the ancient philosopher, "than to hold the lofty and serene positions well fortified by the learning of the wise, from which we may look down upon others and see them wandering all abroad and going astray in their search for the path of life." But who shall say that the citadels of learning are not themselves in danger, when even now in some of our states "truth" is being determined by majority vote?

In any case, this is a humiliating spectacle, and it represents our failure.

Our institutions of higher learning may well be reminded of the words of Washington's *Farewell Address* which express the purpose for which they were established and for which, at least in popular opinion, they are now maintained:

"Promote, then, as an object of prime importance, institutions for the general diffusion of knowledge. In proportion as the structure of a government gives force to public opinion, it is essential that public opinion be enlightened."

This is not to urge for a moment that the universities abate in any degree their activities in specialized research, even though no little of the research which is now carried on in our libraries and our laboratories is like the work of bees in the tropics—storing up honey against a winter which never comes. One may recognize fully the necessity of training specialists for a piece-work civilization; one may be convinced that to extend the frontiers of knowledge is the noblest work of man, and yet plead with our graduate schools to promote a line of research which is now largely if not entirely neglected by them, namely, on the insistent problem of how to bridge the gap between the academic and the public mind, on how to integrate and humanize the scattered fragments of learning for the "enlightenment of public opinion."

However difficult this may be, considering the vast extent and mass of modern knowledge, we know that it can be done, and that the public, including—significant fact—our learned faculties, are waiting, and waiting hungrily, for it to be done. When Professor Thompson covers with sound learning the whole field of science in what he describes correctly as "a plain tale, simply told," a multitude of us marvel at and are grateful for his academic condescension; and when Mr. Wells, though not an authority in the field of historical research, shocks the specialized historians by his ambitious attempt to envisage in two volumes the whole course of human development, he is surprised to find his "Outline" selling better than his novels.

Whether these instances are entirely convincing or not, the manner in which they have been received does reveal a strong popular demand for the "general diffusion of knowledge." To satisfy this at once soundly and effectively requires a combination of comprehensive knowledge and the power to set it at work in human society—a combination now too rarely found. But who dares say that it would not be more common were it encouraged and fostered in the modern university? As things now are, the tempting prizes in the academic world—the highest promotions and the highest salaries—go to the specialist, not to the liberal scholar and teacher. As long as this remains true, we shall, of course, continue to lament the passing of the latter type; for do we not have it on good authority that "where a man's treasure is, there will his heart be also?"

AN ANCIENT REALIST

A number of admirable efforts in recent years to transplant the delicate flowers of the Greek Anthology into the alien soil of English verse [1] may serve to awaken a more general interest in that remarkable collection of Greek minor poetry, which taking its earliest form in the *Garland* of Meleager in the first century B. C., grew from age to age in the hands of various compilers until, in the fourteenth century A. D., Maximus Planudes, a learned monk of Constantinople, included in his up-to-date Anthology verses which are coeval with the beginnings of English Song.

The Anthology as we now have it comprises some five thousand short pieces, which the Greeks called epigrams—a word which means primarily inscriptions on stone, and which was applied to the poems of the Anthology because they were in many cases composed as actual inscriptions or because they purport to be inscriptions, or merely because as literary forms they approach the inscriptional ideal of saying little and suggesting much. They touch upon all manner of themes—love, friendship, family affection, literature, art, religion, nature, the tragedies and comedies of

---

[1] The latest is a collection of verse translations by various authors, including versions of his own, by G. B. Grundy, entitled *Ancient Gems in Modern Settings*, Oxford, 1913.

human life; and it is part of their charm that they often treat these human interests in an intimate and personal way. They range in time over a period of almost nineteen hundred years, from Archilochus, the earliest poet represented in the Anthology, whom we may date roughly at seven hundred B. C., to the latest versifier of the Planudes collection; but the great majority are of the Alexandrian and Byzantine periods. In so vast a mass of poetry, much of it late—mere flickers of dying candles—there is, naturally, a plenty of indifferent verse; but the general average is good, and many, a great many, of these little poems are as perfect in their unpretentious beauty as anything can be.

Some have the prestige of great names—Plato, Sappho or Simonides; some are mere waifs, undated and unclaimed, which have kept their place by intrinsic charm; and still others—and these make up a great number—are by poets who are known from the Anthology alone.

Of the latter poets it is perhaps Leonidas of Tarentum who most deserves to be singled out for special study. He was evidently a favorite with the Greek Anthologists as he was later a favorite of Sainte-Beuve.[2] Meleager praised his verses as the "rich ivy clusters of Leonidas" and wove them prominently into his *Garland*, and it is no accident that in the Anthology which has come down to us Leonidas is represented by a greater number of epigrams than any poet except

[2] *Nouveaux Lundis*, VII, p. 11.

Meleager. Indeed, Meleager is the only one of those whom we may call the humbler poets of the Anthology who could with any justice dispute the supremacy of Leonidas; but as Meleager is par excellence the love poet of the Anthology, and as this is a theme on which Leonidas is all but silent, there is little basis for comparison. It is, perhaps, safe to say that each is superior in his own way. Leonidas could hardly have felt, still less have put into such fervid words, the Romantic passion which in Meleager and his imitators flamed into what Mr. Grundy has boldly called "the most beautiful love-poems in Western literature." [3] He could hardly have written, for example, these lines of Meleager:

> Now the bright crocus flames, and now
> The slim narcissus takes the rain,
> And, straying o'er the mountain's brow
> The daffodillies bud again.
> The thousand blossoms wax and wane
> On wold, and heath, and fragrant bough,
> But fairer than the flowers art thou,
> Than any growth of hill or plain.
> Ye gardens cast your leafy crown,
> That my Love's feet may tread it down,
> Like lilies on the lilies set
> My Love, whose lips are softer far
> Than drowsy poppy petals are,
> And sweeter than the violet! [4]

[3] *Ancient Gems in Modern Settings*, p, xliv.
[4] V. 144, trans. by Andrew Lang.

Leonidas could not have surrendered himself to the Asiatic abandon of these and other characteristic love poems of the later period which, however attractive to modern taste, are nevertheless somewhat un-Hellenic. In the rare instances in which he touches on love it is with the detached interest of one who watches the game, not one who plays it, as in two dedicatory epigrams to Aphrodite, in one of which Callicleia hangs up as thank offerings in the temple of the Goddess a silver Eros, a bronze mirror, and sundry articles of personal embellishment of which she has no further use, having now attained her desire; [5] in the other the handsome Rhodo consecrates to Aphrodite the staff, the sandals, the dirty flask, the tattered wallet containing nothing but ancient philosophy, which seedy old Professor Sochares had owned before they became the spoils of Love.[6]

But the difference between Meleager and Leonidas is not merely one of temperament; it is one of range of interests and sympathy. To Meleager life is love and youthful dalliance, and the only shadows of his world are cast by the somber moods of some lovely Zenophil or Heliodore; Leonidas looks farther and envisages the stern exigencies of the coming years, when life has lost its insouciant vigor and stoops with dull patience to the burdens of Fate. He is oppressed like any Greek by the pathos of human existence, "the riddle of the painful earth," but the characteristic melancholy of his race is in him accentuated by a life of unusual

[5] VI, p. 211.   [6] VI, 293.

stress and trouble. He was born in Tarentum in
Southern Italy; he lived in the early third century
B. C., through the turbulent years of war between
his country and Rome; he saw his people conquered,
himself condemned to wandering exile—"a life that is
no life" he bitterly complains—and cruelest of all, a
grave far from his native land! [7]

Tarentum was but the first of the Greek cities to
feel the shock of Roman arms, and Leonidas' tragic
cry, *bios abios,* "a life that is no life" must have been
raised in many a Greek community throughout the
world as in future years they saw the "wasting War
God of the Italians" [8] advance upon them and over
them with a greed for dominion which appeared to at
least one poet of the Anthology to mock at the limits
of the earth and the sea, and aim at the very heavens
and the citadel of God:

> The mighty throne of the heavens
> Guard, O Zeus, I pray,
> For the earth and the ocean tremble
> Beneath the Roman sway.
>
> The unwearied doors of the highest
> Close, I pray, O God!
> For the road that leads to Olympus
> Is the only road untrod! [9]

"We all dwell in one fatherland, the Universe," and
Meleager,[10] but he was a Syrian by birth and could not

[7] VII, 715.
[8] From Mackail's trans. of Ep. VII, 368.
[9] IX, 576, trans. by Lilla Cabot Perry.
[10] VII, p. 417.

realize that to be a mere citizen of the world was a chill and empty privilege to those who had shared the free life of the old Greek cities which, in the days of their independence, had absorbed the interests, the passions, the ambitions of their members to a degree that we can no longer understand. The breaking up of the solidarity of the old city-state into the larger political unity of the Empire did, in the course of time, result in a thin sentiment of universal brotherhood, but the immediate effect was to rob Greek life of its warming and comforting feeling of social comradeship in all matters of life and death and to fling the individual back upon himself and obsess him with a sense of his aloneness and insignificance. That is why the Anthology is, as Longfellow said of it, one of the saddest of books. Much of the brightness, the warmth, the color which made life so wonderful and death so abhorrent to the Greek race in its youth is now gone from the world, leaving the spirit heavy with the tedium of an existence which is but a painful moment between two eternities:

> Long ere thou sawest the sun,
> Infinite ages had run;
> After the day time is done
> There are infinite years.
>
> Man, what remaineth for thee?
> A point too little to see,
> Or lesser if that may be,
> Thy life time appears.

> Yet evil therein is rife,
> It is filled with sorrow and strife;
> And sweeter by far than life
> Is the death man fears. [11]

These gloomy lines of Leonidas appear to be not merely the expression of a passing mood, as so many pessimistic utterances in Greek literature are, but of a settled melancholy. There is in him little or none of that passionate clinging to life which comes from a feeling that death is the end of all joy in the light of the sun.

> With courage seek the kingdom of the dead,
> The path before you lies:
> It is not hard to find, nor tread;
> No rocks to climb, no lanes to tread;
> But broad and straight, and even still,
> And ever gently slopes down hill;
> You cannot miss it, though you shut your eyes. [12]

Death is better than life; the end, at any rate, is peace. His characters pass off the stage with no regret: Theris, the old fisher, [13] and Platthis, the faithful spinning woman, [14] to their long sleep; Pheidon to the tranquil harbor after a stormy life; [15] old Gorgus, heeding the first call of death and refusing to hoard his weary years:

[11] VII, 472, trans. by J. A. Pott.
[12] IV, 39, trans. by C. Merivale.
[13] VII, 295.
[14] VII, 726.
[15] VII, 478 B.

As on her withered prop doth hang the vine,
So I upon my staff; and death doth call.
Wilt feign thou hearest not, O Soul of mine?
And yet, methinks, thy joy of life were small
To bask in sunshine at hay-harvest tide
Three years or four—were that so sweet to thee?
So calmly musing, Gorgus laid aside
His life and sought the greater company.[16]

Only once does he dwell on the pity of death for the dead; it is in the graceful epitaph which he wrote for the girl-poet Erinna:

"Erinna, young maiden singer among the poets, the bee who gathered the flowers of the Muses, Death snatched away to be his bride. Truly, indeed, did the girl say in her wisdom: 'Thou art envious, O Death!' " [17]

In his other epitaphs, Death is cruel mainly to the living; to the young girl who pining for her dead baby brother goes down with him into the grave; [18] to the heart-stricken mother who would fain follow her dead son but may not:

"Ah, unhappy Anticles, and unhappy I who burned thee on the funeral pyre in the very flower of thy youth, my only son, my child who didst perish at eighteen years! I am left to mourn and lament my lonely old age. O that I might go to shadowy halls of Death; no longer is the dawn sweet to me nor the rays of the keen sun. Ah, unhappy Anticles, cut off

[16] VII, 731, trans. by J. A. Pott.
[17] VII, 13.   [18] VII, 662.

by Fate, be thou the healer of my grief and take me with thee out of life." [19]

In this dreary epitaph, Leonidas shows himself capable of voicing the sorrow which bursts through the reserve of silent pain, but more commonly his sympathy is for those who bear their burdens with uncomplaining acquiescence. He is impressed above all by the hard lot of the poor—patient, laborious days, year upon year, the bent frame, the dim eyes, the withered hands; at last the low, flickering flame, then darkness and eternal night:

> Morning and evening, sleep she drove away—
> Old Platthis—warding hunger from the door;
> And still to wheel and distaff hummed her lay,
> Hard by the gates of Eld, and bent and hoar,
> Plying her loom until the dawn was grey,
> The long course of Athena did she tread;
> With withered hand by withered knee she spun
> Sufficient for the loom of goodly thread;
> Till all her work and all her days were done:
> And in her eightieth year she saw the wave
> Of Acheron—Old Platthis—kind and brave.[20]

> Theris the old, the waves that harvested
> More keen than birds that labor on the sea,
> With spear and net, by shore and rocky bed,
> Not with the well-manned galley labored he.
> Him not the star of storms nor sudden sweep
> Of wind with all his years had smitten and bent;

[19] VII, 37.   [20] VII, 726, trans. by Andrew Lang.

But in his hut of reeds he fell asleep,
As fades a lamp when all the oil is spent.
His tomb nor wife nor children raised, but we,
His fellow toilers, fishers of the sea.[21]

The poet's own life was one of narrow circumstances. In an epigram which is a thank offering for deliverance from sickness, he prays to be released also from the hard straits of poverty; [22] in another, half playful, half sad, he warns the mice to leave his humble cabin and seek a more abundant board:

Dust-loving mouse, go, scamper from my cot!
The meager pantry of Leonidas,
Contenting him, for thee sufficeth not.
Two rolls with salt, such is the fare he has,
Nor asks he better than his father's lot.
What seekest thou then here, thou dainty mouse?
Thou wouldst despise the food whereon I dined.
So hurry off; go try my neighbor's house,
For here is naught; there thou'lt abundance find.[23]

His own experience, then, helped him to a fellow-feeling for the humble toilers who, having bravely waged an unequal war against Fate, claim all the more because they lack the recompense of Elysian Fields the simple "well done" of the living. He has no quarrel with the rich, among whom he doubtless had his friends, nor has he any envy. The facts of the naked-

[21] VII, 295, trans. by Andrew Lang.
[22] VI, 300.
[23] VI, 302, trans. by Lilla Cabot Perry.

ness of birth and of death are too much in his mind
to permit him to be dazzled by the trappings which
are worn between. Old Crethon, once rich in many
lands, now owns his narrow grave, naught else:

> I am the tomb of Crethon; here you read
> His name; himself is numbered with the dead;
> Who once was rich in stable, stall and fold;
> Who once was blest above all living men—
> With lands, how narrow now, how ample then![24]

It is no advantage even to be richly buried. Sufficient is the light covering of a little dust. The lofty
column is but a cruel weight upon the dead.[25] With
these few lines Leonidas dismisses the glamour of
wealth and station and for the rest devotes himself to
"the short and simple annals of the poor:"

> This is the little farm of Cliton: his
> These narrow furrows for the sowing are;
> This little wood for cutting twigs is his,
> And his this somewhat scanty vine. Ah, well!
> Here Cliton passed his four times twenty years.[26]

A number of his epitaphs are for country people,
peasants and shepherds, whose little lives are lent a
lonely pathos by the fact that the world in which they
lived goes on without a pause to mark their absence.
The slab on the grave of poor Alcimines declares that

---

[24] VII, 740, trans. by J. H. Merivale.
[25] VII, 665.
[26] VI, 226, trans. by Lilla Cabot Perry.

this tiny spot of earth belongs to him though now overrun with thorns and brambles which he kept cut while he lived.[27]   Another epitaph, one of the most perfect in the Anthology, pictures the cattle coming home, uncared for, to the steading, while the herdsman, struck by lightning, lies dead beneath the oak tree:

> The hapless cattle from the hillside came,
> Late, and self-herded, beaten on by snow,
> But ah, the herdsman sleepeth, where the flame
> Of heaven beneath the oak tree laid him low.[28]

The above epigram, of which no translation can convey the simple beauty, is claimed for both Leonidas and Diotimus.   There is, however, no doubt about the authorship of the epitaph for the shepherd Clitagoras, in which Mackail finds "all the tenderness of an English pastoral in a land of soft outlines and silvery tones." [29]

> Shepherds that on this mountain ridge abide
> Tending your goats and fleecy flock alway,
> A little favour, but most grateful, pay
> Cleitagoras, nor be the boon denied!
> For sake of mother earth and of the bride
> Of Hades under earth, let sheep, I pray,
> Bleat near me, and the shepherd softly play
> From the scarred rock across the pasture wide.

[27] VII, 656.
[28] VII, 173, trans. by Andrew Lang.
[29] Mackail: *Select Epigrams from the Greek Anthology*, p. 79.

Ah! but in early spring cull meadow-sweet,
Neighbor, and weave a garland for my tomb;
And with ewe's milk be the stone edge bedewed,
When the lambs play about their mother's feet;
So shall you honor well the shades, from whom
Are thanks,—and from the dead is gratitude.[30]

In one of his epigrams, whose earnestness is probably inspired by the dreariness of his own experience,[31]
Leonidas warns men against the homeless life of those
who wander over seas from land to land; better a little hut for shelter, a tiny hearth, and scant, coarse
fare.[32] And yet he feels at times, like any member of
the race which made the *Odyssey*, the alluring call of
the sea:

'Tis time to sail! The chattering swallow's come;
There blows a pleasant breeze from out the west;
The meadows now are springing into bloom;
The sea, once-storm-tossed, now has sunk to rest.
So weigh the anchor! let the cable run!
And sail away with all your canvas set!
The God of all the harbours says "Begone,
And fare ye forth your livelihood to get!" [33]

However, the sailor's life was not always one of
summer skies and smiling waves; among a sea-going
people, many were constrained by poverty or other
causes to voyage in frail ships through the winter sea-

[30] VII, 637, trans. by William H. Hardinge.
[31] VII, 715.
[32] VII, 736.
[33] X, 1, trans. by G. B. Grundy.

son when the ocean was frequently swept by sudden violent storms. To them, "even as a mother is sweeter than a step-mother, the land was dearer than the hoary sea." [34] It was a perilous business and too often the waves took their toll of death. The ghastly desolateness of such a fate is a common theme of the Anthology, and a number of the epigrams of Leonidas express his shuddering pity of those who go down in the cold and the dark:

"A rough and steep-down squall out of the East and night and the waves of the gloomy setting of Orion were my bane, and I, Callaeschrus, lost my hold of life as I sped through the mid Libyan sea: So I am rolled drifting in the ocean to be the prey of fishes, and this stone says falsely that is over me." [35]

Another sailor was more fortunate in that his body was washed upon the shore to be tended by loving hands and placed within a grave!

"Do not set sail trusting in a long ship or deep; one storm is stronger than any ship afloat. A single gale destroyed Promachus and the sudden wave swept his sailors into the yawning sea. Yet fate was not altogether cruel to him; on his native soil he won a tomb and funeral rites at the hands of his kin; for the rough sea had deposited his body on the wide-spreading shore." [36]

Another complains that he lives too near the hated sea which had done him to death:

[34] IX, 23.
[35] VII, 273, trans. by Mackail. Cf. VII, 652.
[36] VII, 665.

"Tumultuous sea, having handled me so cruelly, why didst thou not spew me forth far from the dreary shore? Then would I not, now that I am clothed about with the dark mist of death, be so near neighbor to thee." [37]

The feeling of the hostility and cruelty of the sea which appears in so many of the sailor epitaphs of the Anthology is shared also by fisher folk, who after years of precarious struggle against a treacherous element are in the end overwhelmed by a sense of its brutishness:

> Around his fisher's spear he tied his net,
> Ceasing from toil upon the weary sea;
> With silent tears his aged eyes were wet,
> As, turning to Poseidon, thus spake he:
> "I'm weary, blessed one, and nigh to death,
> But poverty alas! is ever young!
> So while a poor old man still draws his breath,
> Oh, give him sustenance, my lord, but wrung
>
> From out the land, and not from out the sea,
> It, as 'tis said, of both thou ruler be." [38]

The same weariness expressed with more restraint is found in the epigram of Leonidas in which the old fisher Diophantus dedicates to the God of the Sea his hooks, his line, his long rods, his creels, his fish

[37] VII, 283.
[38] VI, by Macedonius but in the manner of Leonidas. Trans. by G. B. Grundy.

trap, his three-pronged spear, his two oars—all that he has left to show from his ancient craft.[39]

In the epitaph which Leonidas wrote for himself, anticipating his own death, he says after speaking of his unhappy life, "but the Muses loved me and I have this sweetness in my bitter lot. The name of Leonidas is not fallen into oblivion; the gifts of the Muses alone proclaim it as long as suns rise and set." [40]

Did Leonidas base this confidence of immortal fame upon such slender "gifts of the Muses" as the Anthology brings to us? Or was he the author of poems of a more ambitious kind, and is it a mere accident that only epigrams have come down to us under his name? There is good reason to believe that the twenty-first poem published among the idyls of Theocritus was not written by Theocritus but by Leonidas. It has none of the marks of Theocritus, but shows many of Leonidas' qualities and tricks of style. It is a vivid picture of the poor and simple life of fisherfolk, and is characterized by the sympathetic realism of the fisher epigrams of Leonidas. It betrays the same fondness for the detailed enumeration of the implements of the craft which appears in a number of Leonidas' epigrams, notably in the last one cited,[41] and is, moreover, addressed to Diophantus, the name of the old fisherman who in the above epigram dedicates all his gear to Poseidon. But the poem will make its own argument. It opens with a brief dedication to Diophantus, which is in the form of a general reflection upon the

disquieting effects of poverty. Then follows a picture
of two old fishermen sleeping side by side in their poor
cabin by the sea, with the tools and instruments of their
craft strewn all about them. Before the night is half
spent, worry for the morrow breaks their sleep, and
they while away the hours before the dawn with talk.
One tells the other of a marvelous dream in which he
had caught a fish of gold; thinking himself a rich
man, he had vowed to Poseidon in the dream that
henceforth he would desert the sea and live on the
land. The oath troubles him until his companion reas-
sures him by telling him that the oath which he swore
was no more real than the fish he caught, and that he
had better turn his attention to actual fishing lest he
starve on his golden dreams:

" 'Tis poverty alone, Diophantus, that awakens the
arts; Poverty, the very teacher of labor. Nay, not
even sleep is permitted, by weary cares, to men that
live by toil, and if, for a little while, one close his eyes
in the night, cares throng about him, and suddenly dis-
quiet his slumber.

Two fishers, on a time, two old men, together lay
and slept; they had strown the dry sea-moss for a bed
in their wattled cabin, and there they lay against the
leafy wall. Beside them were strewn the instruments
of their toilsome hands, the fishing-creels, the rods of
reed, the hooks, the sails bedraggled with sea-spoil, the
lines, the reels, the lobster pots woven of rushes, the
seines, two oars, and an old coble upon props. Beneath their heads was a scanty matting, their clothes,

their sailor's caps. Here was all their toil, here all
their wealth. The threshold had never a door, nor a
watch-dog; all things, all, to them seemed superfluity,
for Poverty was their sentinel. They had no neighbor by them, but ever against their narrow cabin
gently floated up the sea.

The chariot of the moon had not yet reached the
midpoint of her course, but their familiar toil
awakened the fishermen; from their eyelids they cast
out slumber, and roused their souls with speech.

ASPHALION.—They lie all, my friend, who say that
the nights wane short in summer, when Zeus brings
the long days. Already have I seen ten thousand
dreams, and the dawn is not yet. Am I wrong, what
ails them, the nights are surely long?

THE FRIEND.—Asphalion, thou blamest the beautiful summer! It is not that the season hath willfully
passed his natural course, but care, breaking thy sleep,
makes night seem long to thee.

ASPHALION.—Didst ever learn to interpret dreams?
for good dreams have I beheld, I would not have thee
to go without thy share in my vision; even as we go
shares in the fish we catch, so share all my dreams!
Sure, thou art not to be surpassed in wisdom; and he
is the best interpreter of dreams that hath wisdom for
his teacher. Moreover, we have time to idle in, for
what could a man find to do, lying on a leafy bed beside the wave and slumbering not?

THE FRIEND.—Tell me, then, the vision of the
night; nay, tell all to thy friend.

ASPHALION.—As I was sleeping late, amid the labors of the salt sea (and truly not too full-fed, for we supped early if thou dost remember, and did not over-task our bellies), I saw myself busy on a rock, and there I sat and watched the fishes, and kept spinning the bait with the rods. And one of the fish nibbled, a fat one, for in sleep dogs dream of bear, and of fish dream I. Well, he was tightly hooked, and the blood was running, and the rod I grasped was bent with the struggle. So with both hands I strained, and had a sore tussle for the monster. How was I ever to land so big a fish with hooks all too slim? Then just to remind him he was hooked, I gently pricked him, pricked, and slackened, and, as he did not run, I took in line. My toil was ended with the sight of my prize; I drew up a golden fish, lo you, a fish all plated thick with gold! Then fear took hold of me, lest he might be some fish beloved of Poesidon, or perchance some jewel of the sea-grey Amphitrite. Gently I unhooked him, lest ever the hooks should retain some of the gold of his mouth. Then I dragged him on shore with the ropes, and swore that never again would I set foot on sea, but abide on land, and lord it over the gold.

This was even what wakened me, but, for the rest, set thy mind to it, my friend, for I am in dismay about the oath I swore.

THE FRIEND.—Nay, never fear, thou art no more sworn than thou hast found the golden fish of thy vision; dreams are but lies. But if thou wilt search these waters, wide awake, and not asleep, there is some hope in thy slumbers; seek the fish of flesh, lest thou die of famine with all thy dreams of gold!" [42]

The Muse of Leonidas has many moods, playful and bright as well as sad. He is indeed, as Sainte-Beuve pointed out, the most representative poet of the Anthology,[43] but that which distinguishes him from all the rest, and which appears in the idyl of the fisherman as in his epigrams, is his sympathy for the poor—their incessant struggle against want, the patience and the courage of their narrow lives.

[42] Trans. by Andrew Lang.

[43] S' étant essayé avec succès dans la plupart des genres, excepté le tendre, il nous sera comme un abrégé vivant de l'Anthologie, dans sa partie du moins la plus honorable et la plus digne. *Nouveaux Lundis,* VII, p. 11.

THE CONVENTIONS OF THE PASTORAL ELEGY

The influence of the Greek and Latin Classics on the literature of Modern Europe is nowhere so definitely illustrated as in the history of pastoral poetry. The haunting melodies of the Greek pastoral and their graceful echoes in the *Eclogues* of Virgil have exercised a charm so captivating to later poets in this field that not only the general framework of the Classical models, but their very turns of phrase and tricks of style, and even the musical names they give to their rustic characters, have persisted through centuries of pastoral song.[1] I propose in this paper to point out the most striking illustrations of the Classical influence in the conventions which occur most frequently in a single form of the pastoral—the pastoral elegy or dirge, a lament for the death, the absence or the loss of one beloved.

The Greek examples are Theocritus' Woes of

[1] "In Pastoralism, literary tradition penetrates everywhere, like an atmosphere, softening the asperities of innovation and touching the contours even of work fashioned by a Shakespeare or a Milton with a halo of allusion and reminiscence" (C. H. Herford, in Preface to *English Pastorals*). Cf. the illustrative material collected in Professor Mustard's "Later Echoes of the Greek Bucolic Poets," *American Journal of Philology*, XXX, pp. 245-283. I am indebted to this article, and more directly to the kindness of Professor Mustard, for valuable suggestions.

Daphnis, in the first Idyll, Bion's Death of Adonis, and Moschus' Lament for Bion; for Latin literature, we have Virgil's fifth and tenth Eclogues.[2] The publication of the editio princeps of Theocritus in Milan, in 1481, and the Aldine edition, which contained also the elegies of Bion and Moschus, in 1495, started the fashion of singing the loss of kin or friend in musical numbers studiously echoed from the dirges of Theocritus, Bion, Moschus and Virgil. In Italy, the late Fifteenth and the Sixteenth Century saw a surfeit of such elegies, composed now in Latin, now in Italian verse.[3] From Italy the fashion spread to Spain, where in the early Sixteenth Century this form was cultivated by Garcilaso de la Vega.[4]

In France, about the same time (1531) Clément Marot published his masterpiece—a pastoral elegy on the death of Madame Loyse de Savoye, one of the most highly finished and elaborate of the modern dirges.

[2] The first eclogue of Nemesianus is an elegy of a sort, but it seems to have played little or no part in the tradition of the pastoral lament. The medieval lament for Adalhard, Abbot of Corbeil (by Paschasius Radbertus), has recently been discussed by J. H. Hanford, *Publications of the Modern Language Association*, XXV (1910), p. 427.

[3] I shall limit myself here to the more notable examples, those of Pontano, Sannazaro, Luigi Alamanni and Tasso. Pontano's Meliseus, a Latin eclogue in which he laments the death of his wife, is modeled after Virgil's fifth eclogue, but shows acquaintance with Moschus. Sannazaro's Phyllis, a lament in Latin for Carmosina, is also patterned freely after Virgil but in the eleventh eclogue of the Arcadia he does little more than paraphrase the dirge of Moschus. Alamanni's first two eclogues, laments for his friend Rucellai, are paraphrased respectively from Theocritus' first Idyll and Moschus' Death of Bion. His tenth eclogue imitates closely Bion's dirge. Tasso's Rogo di Corinna abounds in echoes from Theocritus, Bion, Moschus and Virgil.

[4] His first two eclogues contain elegies of the conventional type.

This poem was followed very closely as the model of Spenser's *November;* and from this time on the pastoral elegy was as popular in England as it had been in Italy.[5]

The Pastoral Masquerade [6]

The distinguishing characteristic of the pastoral elegy is that its subject masquerades as a herdsman moving amid rustic scenes, as, for example, in Matthew Arnold's *Thyrsis,* where the restless temperament and troubled life of his poet friend become in pastoral metaphor:

He loved each simple joy the country yields,
　　He loved his mates; but yet he could not keep,
For that a shadow lour'd on the fields,
　　Here with the shepherds and the silly sheep.
　　　Some life of men unblest
He knew, which made him droop, and fill'd his head.
　　He went; his piping took a troubled sound
　　Of storms that rage outside our happy ground;
He could not wait their passing, he is dead.

[5] Of the many instances of it in English, the following, which I mention in chronological order, are, perhaps, of greatest interest: the pastoral elegies by "A. W.," and by Francis Davison, published in Davison's *Poetical Rhapsody;* Spenser's Astrophel; Thomas Watson, Meliboeus; Drayton, Eclogue IV of the Shepheard's Garland; William Browne, A Dirge, and Death of Philarete; William Drummond, Damon's Lament, and Pastoral Elegy on the death of Sir William Alexander; Ben Jonson, Aeglamour's Lament; Milton, Lycidas; Pope, Fourth Pastoral; Ambrose Philips, Albino; John Gay, Friday, or the Dirge; Shelley, Adonais; Matthew Arnold, Thyrsis. The tradition is continued freely in Reginald Fanshawe's Corydon, an Elegy in Memory of Matthew Arnold and Oxford.
[6] Ἦς δ'αἰπόλος . . αἰπόλῳ ἔξοχ' ἐ ᾤκει (Theoc.).

This convention begins with Moschus. In the earliest example, the dirge of Theocritus, the subject of the song is really a herdsman and the dirge of Theocritus is perhaps little more than an idealized version of folk-songs he had heard Sicilian shepherds sing in honor of their rustic hero. The Adonis of Bion's elegy is also a shepherd divinity; but when we come to Moschus, the hero of the song is no longer a shepherd but the poet Bion, whose only connection with the pastoral life is that he wrote verses in the pastoral vein. Moschus adopts the form of Theocritus and Bion, and frankly makes a shepherd of his poet hero. Here we have for the first time, as Chambers [7] puts it, the pastoral form used to "express in poetic metaphor the sorrow of those who loved a singer and a friend. In our own literature it has become traditional for such a purpose. Again and again throughout the centuries

> The same sweet cry no circling seas can drown
> In melancholy cadence rose to swell
> Some dirge of Lycidas or Astrophel,
> When lovely souls and pure, before their time,
> Into the dusk went down.

Philip Sidney and Edward King, John Keats and Arthur Clough, all alike cut off by an ineluctable fate in the flower of their days; for all alike the cadences of a half forgotten Greek poet have woven their imperishable memorial."

[7] *English Pastorals*, "Introduction," p. xliii.

Frame-work of The Elegy

The dirge of Theocritus is preceded by a dramatic introduction. Two herdsmen interchange mutual compliments, and one is induced by flattery and the promise of a gift to sing the "Woes of Daphnis." After the dirge there is further talk, praise of the singer, and at the end a return to the commonplace of present reality. This is essentially the plan of Virgil's fifth eclogue, of the Latin dirges of Pontano and Sannazaro, of Alamanni's first eclogue, of Tasso's Rogo di Corinna, first part, of the Elegies of Garcilaso de la Vega, of Marot's Complainte de Madame Loyse de Savoye, of Spenser's November, of the pastoral elegies of Pope, Philips and Gay. The dirges of Bion and Moschus and Virgil's tenth eclogue lack this dramatic setting, and plunge at once into the theme or approach it by a short prelude or invocation. So, also, a number of modern dirges; for example, Sannazaro's Arcadia, eleventh eclogue, Almanni's second eclogue, Milton's Lycidas, Shelley's Adonais, M. Arnold's Thyrsis.

Refrain

A striking feature of the dirge of Theocritus is the refrain:

ἄρχετε βουκολικᾶς Μοῖσαι φίλαι, ἄρχετ' ἀοιδᾶς

Bion also uses it:

αἰάζω τὸν Ἄδωνιν 'ἀπώλετο καλὸς Ἄδωνις':

and Moschus:

ἄρχετε Σικελικαί, τῷ πένθεος ἄρχετε Μοῖσαι.

The modern dirge employs it often: Sannazaro, Arcadia, Ecl. XI, "Ricominciate, Muse, il vostro pianto"; Alamanni, Ecl. I, "Date principio, o Muse, al tristo canto"; Ecl. II, "Piangete sempre homai, Sorelle Tosche"; Ecl. X, "Piangiamo Adon, che'l bello Adone è morto"; Tasso, Corinna (closing song), "Piangete, antiche Ninfe"; Garcilaso, Ecl. I (Salicio's song), "Salid sin duelo, lágrimas, corriendo"; Marot, "Chantez, mes vers, chantez"; Spenser, November, "O heavie herse! . . . O carefull verse!"; Milton, Epitaphium Damonis, "Ite domum impasti, domino iam non vacat, agni"; Pope, Fourth Pastoral, "Fair Daphne's dead and Beauty is no more"; Third Pastoral, "Resound ye hills, resound my mournful strain."

All Nature Mourns

The appeal to Nature to mourn or the representation of Nature as sharing in the universal sorrow is a commonplace almost never absent from the pastoral dirge. In Theocritus, the mountains and trees mourned for Daphnis. In Bion's elegy, mountains, trees, springs and rivers share in Aphrodite's sorrow for the lost Adonis, and the flowers flush red with pain. So in Moschus, all the flowers withered and the trees cast down their fruit for grief when Bion died. In Virgil's tenth eclogue, "the laurels and the tamarisks wept for Gallus, Mount Maenalus crowned with pines bemoaned

him, and the rocks of chill Lycaeus." In the modern
dirge this convention is employed often with extreme
elaboration. Generally speaking, the ancient poets
have "sowed with the hand, the modern, with the
sack." [8] The dirge of Pontanus, some two hundred
and fifty lines, is made up almost entirely of it,[9] and
many later elegies are overcharged with Nature's tears
and groans.[10] Of the saner uses of this "pathetic
fallacy" I quote two examples, Spenser, November,
who echoes Marot and Moschus:

Ay me! that dreerie Death should strike so mortall stroke,
That can undoe Dame Nature's kindly course;
The faded lockes fall from the loftie oak,
The flouds do gaspe, for dryed is theyr sourse,
And flouds of teares flowe in theyr stead perforse;
    The mantled medowes mourne,
    Theyr sondry colours tourne.

[8] Moschus was the first to overdo it and is responsible, largely, for
the sins of modern excess.

[9] I quote a sample:
> En squalent prata et sua sunt sine honore salicta,
> Extinctamque Ariadman agri, Ariadnan et ipsae
> Cum gemitu referunt silvae, vallesque queruntur.
> Extinctamque Ariadnam iterant clamantia saxa,
> Et colles iterant Ariadnam, Ariadnam et amnes.

[10] Baptista Mantuanus, Ecl. III, contents himself with a reference
to Ovid and Virgil:
> te Padus et noster lugubri Mincius ore
> cum Nymphis flevere suis, ut Thracius Hebrus
> Orphea; te tristes ovium flevere magistri,
> ut Daphnim luxisse ferunt; te pascua et agri
> undique; et audita est totis querimonia campis.

(*The Eclogues of Baptista Mantuanus, ed.* W. P. Mustard, Bal-
timore, 1911, p. 129.)

O heavie herse!
The heavens doe melt in teares without remorse;
    O carefull verse!

and Shelley, Adonais:

All he had loved, and moulded into thought,
From shape, and hue, and odour, and sweet sound,
Lamented Adonais. Morning sought
Her eastern watch-tower, and her hair unbound,
Wet with the tears which should adorn the ground,
Dimmed the aerial eyes that kindle day;
Afar the melancholy thunder moaned,
Pale Ocean in unquiet slumber lay,
And the wild Winds flew round, sobbing in their dismay.

Grief made the young Spring wild, and she threw down
Her kindling buds, as if she Autumn were,
Or they dead leaves; since her delight is flown,
For whom should she have waked the sullen year?

In many cases Nature is challenged to reverse her usual course and let confusion reign. This convention begins with Theocritus: "Now bear violets ye brambles, bear violets ye thorns, and let the beautiful narcissus flower on the boughs of the juniper! Let all things with one another be confounded; let the pine tree bear pears since Daphnis is dying; let the stag drag down the hounds, and let owls from the hills vie with nightingales in song." So Pontanus, imitating Virgil's echo of this passage:

Dira lues coelo ruat, et ruat altus Olympus.
Stragem agris, stragem arboribus, terraeque ruinam

Det super et mediis tellus internatet undis.
Non uxor mihi cara domi.

Tasso, Rogo di Corinna, makes much of it:

Stelle, stelle crudeli,
Perchè non mi celate il vostro lume,
Poi che il suo m'ascondeste?
Perchè non volgi, o Luna, addietro 'l corso?
Perchè non copre intorno orrido nembo
Il tuo dolce sereno?
Perchè il ciel non si tigne
Tutto di nere macchie e di sanguigne?
Tenebre, o voi che le serene luci
M'ingombraste repente,
Coprite il cielo e i suoi spietati lumi,
E minaccino sol baleni e lampi
D'ardere il mondo e le celesti spere.
Stíasi dolente ascoso il Sol nell' onde;
Tema natura di perpetua notte;
Tremi la terra; ed Aquilone ed Austro
Facciano insieme impetuosa guerra,
Crollando i boschi, e le robuste piante
Svelte a terra spargendo; il mar si gonfi,
E con onde spumanti il lido ingombri;
Volgano i fiumi incontro ai fonti il corso.

Virgil, Eclogue V, complains of the decline of Nature's kindly powers: "Since the fates have reft us of thee (Daphnis), Pales and Apollo have themselves abandoned the fields. In the furrows to which we

often entrusted the large barley seed, the accursed
darnel and barren wild oats only spring. In place of
the soft violet and the purple narcissus, rise the thistle
and the thorn." This passage is echoed again and
again. Garcilaso imitates it at some length, Ecl. I:

> Despues que nos dejaste nunca pace
> En hartura el ganado ya, ni acude
> El campo al labrador con mano llena.
>
> .   .   .   .   .   .
>
> La tierra que de buena
> Gana nos producía
> Flores con que solía
> Quitar en solo vellas mil enojos,
> Produce agora en cambio estos abrojos,
> Ya de rigor de espinas intratable;
> Y yo hago con mis ojos
> Crecer llorando el fruto miserable.

Also Tasso, Corinna:

> Posciache t'involò l'acerba morte,
> Pale medesma abbandonò piangendo
> Le sue nude campagne, e seco Apollo:
> E nei solchi, in cui già fu sparso il grano,
> Vi signoreggia l'infelice loglio,
> E la sterile avena, o felce appresso
> Sventurata che frutto non produce;
> E in vece pur di violetta molle,
> Di purpureo narciso e di giacinto,
> Il cardo sorge.

And Ambrose Philips, Albino:

> Since thou delicious youth didst quit the plains,
> The ungrateful ground we till with fruitless pains,
> In laboured furrows sow the choice of wheat
> And over empty sheaves in harvest sweat.
> A thin increase our fleecy cattle yield
> And thorns and thistles overspread the field.

Ben Jonson, Aeglamour's Lament, uses the convention with more originality:

> A spring, now she is dead! of what? of thorns,
> Briars and brambles? thistles, burs and docks?
> Cold hemlock, yew? the mandrake or the box?
> These may grow still; but what can spring beside?
> Did not the whole earth sicken when she died?
> As if there since did fall one drop of dew
> But what was wept for her! or any stock
> Did bear a flower, or any branch a bloom,
> After her wreath was made.

The beasts of field and forest also show their grief, especially the herds and flocks now left to roam without a shepherd. In Theocritus, the "jackals and the wolves cried for Daphnis; for him even the lion from the forest made lament; his bulls and kine with their young calves bewailed him." In Bion, the hounds of Adonis set up a woeful cry, and in Moschus, the herds of Bion refuse to graze. In Virgil's fifth Eclogue: "No shepherd pastured the herd, after the death of Daphnis, or drove it to the cool stream; no four-footed thing would taste of the river or touch the grassy sward." This becomes an almost universal convention in the later pastoral. For example, Pontanus:

> Pastores Ariadnam, Ariadnam armenta querantur
> Extinctamque Ariadnam opacis buccula silvis
> Cum gemitu testetur;

Spenser, November:

> The feeble flocks in field refuse their former foode,
> And hang theyr heads as they would learne to weepe;
> The beastes in forest wayle as they were woode,
>
> .   .   .   .
>
> Now she is gone that safely did hem keepe;

Ambrose Phillips:

> No cattle grazed the field nor drank the flood.
> Bleating around him lie his plaintive sheep.[11]

[11] Cf. the burlesque in Gay's Friday:

> When Blouzelind expired, the wether's bell
> Before the drooping flock tolled forth her knell;
> The solemn death watch clicked the hour she died,
> And shrilling crickets in the chimney cried . . .
> The lambkin which her wonted tendance bred
> Dropped on the plains that fatal instant dead.

The most interesting use of this convention is in Shelley's Adonais:

> Oh weep for Adonais! . . . The quick Dreams,
> The passion-winged Ministers of thought,
> *Who were his flocks,* whom near the living streams
> Of his young spirit he fed, and whom he taught
> The love which was its music, wander not, . . .

Wander no more, from kindling brain to brain,
But droop there, whence they sprung; and mourn their lot
Round the cold heart, where, after their sweet pain,
They ne'er will gather strength, or find a home again.

"Where Were Ye, Nymphs?"

The legendary Daphnis of Theocritus is the son of
Hermes and a nymph. His childhood was passed
among the nymphs, who brought him up. Thyrsis
complains that they were not present when Daphnis
was dying: "Where were ye, Nymphs, when Daphnis
was wasting in death—O, where were ye? In Peneus'
beautiful vales or in the vales of Pindus? For
surely ye dwelt not by the great river Anapus nor
on the watch-tower of Aetna nor by the sacred waters
of Acis." This perfectly natural reproach in Theocritus becomes one of the most artificial conventions in the pastoral dirge. Virgil imitates it very
closely in the tenth eclogue: "In what woods or
glades were ye, Naiad Nymphs, when Gallus was dying
of love? For not on Parnassus' slopes did ye linger,
nor on the slopes of Pindus, nor by Aonian Aganippe."

So Luigi Alamanni, Ecl. I:

> Ov' eran tutte allor Grazie et Virtuti?
> Ove voi, Muse, allor che la chiara alma
> Del divin Cosmo al summo ciel salìo?
> Non già non già lungo le fresche rive
> Del suo chiaro Arno, e non fra i verdi colli
> Del suo fiorito nido; anzi lontane

> Foste allor si, che tardo fu'l soccorso
> Di tôrre a morte quel cui tanto amaste.

Garcilaso, Ecl. I, imitates more freely:

> Inexorable Diosa demandabas
> En aquel paso ayuda;
> Y tú, rústica Diosa, dónde estabas?
> Ibate tanto en perseguir las fieras?

Marot's elegy has a slight echo:

> Que faictes vous en ceste forest verte
> Faunes, Sylvains? je croy que dormez là;
> Veillez, veillez, pour plorer ceste perte.

Baïf, Ecl. II, Brinon, patterned after Virgil, Ecl. X, has an elaborate imitation, of which I quote the beginning:

> Nymphes, quel mont lointain, quelle forest ombreus
> Quel fleuve, quel rocher, quelle caverne creuse
> Vos detint?

This becomes in Spenser's Astrophel:

> Ah! where were ye this while, his shepheard peares,
> To whom alive was nought so deare as hee?
> And ye faire mayds, the matches of his yeares,
> Which in his grace did boast you most to bee;
> Ah! where were ye, when he of you had need.
> To stop his wound that wondrously did bleed?

Milton's Lycidas studiously echoes the classical models:

> Where were ye, Nymphs, when the remorseless deep
> Closed o'er the head of your loved Lycidas?
> For neither were ye playing on the steep
> Where your old bards, the famous Druids, lie,
> Nor on the shaggy top of Mona high,
> Nor yet where Deva spreads her wizard stream.

Also Pope's Second Pastoral:

> Where stray ye, Muses, in what lawn or grove,
> While Corydon thus pines in hopeless love,
> In these fair fields where sacred Isis glides
> Or else where Cam his winding vales divides?

Shelley's rendering is more free:

> Where were thou, mighty Mother, when he lay,
> When thy Son lay, pierced by the shaft which flies
> In darkness? Where was lorn Urania
> When Adonais died?

"The Mountain Shepherds Came."

I have already said that the Daphnis of Theocritus is of divine origin, the son of Hermes and a nymph. So Hermes naturally comes to Daphnis when he is dying, and asks him the cause of his torment. The neat-herds come, and the shepherds; the rustic Priapus also comes. All say, "Unhappy Daphnis, wherefore dost thou languish?" This also becomes a very artificial formula. Virgil imitates it in the tenth Eclogue. Shepherds and swineherds, Menacles among them, come to Gallus and ask, "Whence this love of yours?"

Apollo comes and questions, "Gallus, why so mad?"
Silvanus also comes, and Pan; all ask, "Will you ever
put bounds to your tears?"

Alamanni, Ecl. I, imitates Theocritus:

> Discese Apollo a noi dal suo Parnaso
> Et piangendo dicea; deh, miser Cosmo,
> Dov' or ten vai?   Chi de te 'l mondo spoglia?
> Pan venne poi con mille altri pastori, etc.

Also Garcilaso, Ecl. II:

> Vinieron los pastores de ganados;
> Vinieron de los sotos los vaqueros,
> Para ser de mi mal de mi informados.
> Y todos con los gestos lastimeros
> Me preguntaban, quáles habian sido
> Los accidentes de mi mal primeros.

Marot has a somewhat fainter echo:

> Nymphes et dieux de nuict en grand' destresse
> La vindrent veoir.

Baïf, Ecl. II, in the passage beginning:

> Tous les Dieux qui des chams ont le soin et la garde
> Viennent de toutes pars,

expands the convention into fifty-four lines.

Milton, Lycidas, elaborates it into the curiously
involved passage beginning:

> But now my oat proceeds
> And listens to the Herald of the Sea,

That came in Neptune's plea.
He asked the waves, and asked the felon winds,
What hard mishap hath doomed this gentle swain.

More simply, Shelley, Adonais:

                    and the mountain shepherds came,
Their garlands sere, their magic mantles rent;
The Pilgrim of Eternity, whose fame
Over his living head like heaven is bent,
An early but enduring monument,
Came, veiling all the lightnings of his song
In sorrow. From her wilds Ierne sent
The sweetest lyrist of her saddest wrong,
And love taught grief to fall like music from his tongue.

'Midst others of less note came one frail Form, etc.

"With Fairest Flowers . . . I'll Sweeten Thy Sad Grave"

The command to deck the bier or the grave
of the dead with garlands, or the representation of
friends of the dead bringing flowers, occurs frequently.
The tradition begins with Bion, where Aphrodite is enjoined to deck the bier of Adonis with flowers and
wreaths, βάλλε δε νιν στεφάνοισι καὶ ἄνθεσι. In Virgil's fifth
eclogue the singer requests the shepherds to strew the
ground with leaves and plant shade-giving trees about
Daphnis' tomb:

Spargite humum foliis, inducite fontibus umbras. . .
Et tumulum facite.

Of this there are many brief echoes, as in Baptista
Mantuanus, Ecl. III:

Spargite, pastores, tumulum redolentibus herbis;

Castiglione, Alcon:

Vos mecum, o pueri, bene olentes spargite flores,
Narcissum atque rosas et suave rubentem hyacinthum,
Atque umbras hedera lauroque inducite opacas:
Nec desint casiae permixtaque cinnama amomo,
Excitet ut dulces aspirans ventus odores.

Sannazaro, Phyllis:

tu coniferas ad busta cupressus
Sparge manu et viridi tumulum super intege myrto;

Tasso, Corinna:

Di verdi fronde voi l'arida terra,
O pastori, spargete: . . .
Fate il sepolcro, etc.

Pontano elaborates it somewhat:

Legite intactos et jungite flores
et solis luctum et pueri lachrymantis amorem.
Legite et abscissos Veneris de fronte capillos
Post ubi io Ariadnan io Ariadnan, et ipsum
Implestis clamore nemus, hunc addite honorem
Ad tumulum, pia verba acrem testantia luctum.

Marot turns it into a passage of lingering sweetness:

> Portez rameaulx parvenuz à croissance;
> Laurier, lyerre et lys blancs honorez,
> Romarin vert, roses en abondance,
> Jaune soucie et bassinetz dorez,
> Passeveloux de pourpre colorez,
> Lavende franche, oeilletz de couleur vive,
> Aubepins blancs, aubepins azurez,
> Et toutes fleurs de grand' beauté nayfve.
> Chascune soit d'en porter attentive,
> Puis sur la tumbe en jectez bien espais,
> Et n'oubliez force branches d'olive,
> Car elle estoit la bergere de paix.

From the English pastoral I cite two examples, William Drummond, Elegy on the Death of Sir William Alexander:

> Fair nymphs, the blushing hyacinth and rose
> Spread on the place his relics doth enclose;
> Weave garlands to his memory, and put
> Over his hearse, a verse in cypress cut,

and the exquisite flower scene of Milton's Lycidas:

> And call the vales, and bid them hither cast
> Their bells and flowerets of a thousand hues.
> .   .   .   .
> To strew the laureate hearse where Lycid lies.

"The Riddle Of This Painful Earth"

There is expressed in almost every dirge, ancient or modern, a feeling of bitter resentment against the cruel

fate which blasts life in the bud or cuts it off in the fullness of its flower.[12]   Sometimes this is expressed as in
the words Bion gives to Aphrodite: "Far thou fliest
from me, Adonis.   To Acheron thou goest, the loathed
and cruel king of death.   But I, unhappy, live, for I
am a goddess and may not follow thee.   Take thou
my lord, Persephone, for thou art stronger than I, and
all things fair descend to thee."

Compare Tasso, Corinna:

> Oh dolore, oh pietate!
> Oh miseria del mondo!
> Come passa repente e come fugge
> Virtù, grazia, bellezza e leggiadrìa!

William Drummond, Pastoral Elegy on the Death of
Sir William Alexander:

> O death, what treasure in one hour
> Hast thou dispersed; how dost thou devour
> What we on earth hold dearest!   All things good,
> Too envious Heavens, how blast ye in the bud!

and Shelley, Adonais:

> For he is gone where all things wise and fair
> Descend.   Oh dream not that the amorous deep
> Will yet restore him to the vital air!

Death feeds on his mute voice, and laughs at our despair.

---

[12] Andrelinus, Menalcas: "invicta resecat mors improba falce."
Lady Pembroke, Astrophel: "What cruel hand of cursed foe un-
                                     known
                                     Hath cropped the stalk which bore
                                     so fair a flower?"
Milton, Lycidas: "Comes the blind Fury with the
                                     abhorred shears."

Sometimes the complaint is against the Heavens which allow such things to be, as in Virgil's fifth eclogue, where Daphnis' mother, clasping the dead body of her son, upbraids the gods and the stars for their cruelty. So Ambrose Phillips, in close imitation of Virgil:

> The pious mother comes with grief oppress'd:
> Ye trees and conscious fountains can attest
> With what sad accents, and what piercing cries,
> She filled the grove and importuned the skies,
> And every star upbraided with his death,
> When in her widowed arms, devoid of breath,
> She clasped her son.

Oftentimes the melancholy mood born of the sense of bereavement expresses itself in the form of a contrast drawn between the immortality of Nature's life and the mortality of man. "There is hope of a tree if it be cut down, that it will sprout again and that the tender branch will not cease. . . . But man dieth and wasteth away. Yea, man giveth up the ghost and where is he?" The earliest instance of this in the pastoral occurs in the splendid lines of Moschus' elegy: "Ah me! the mallows when they fade and perish in the garden, and the green parsley and the fair-flowering tendrils of the anise, they awake to life again and grow, with the coming of another spring. But we, the human kind, the great, the mighty and the wise, when once we die, unheeding in the hollow earth we sleep . . . the long endless, never waking sleep." This contrast is one of the most natural and one of the most effective features of the dirge, and it is not surprising that it becomes one of the most striking conventions of the modern pastoral elegy. Here it occurs first in Sannazaro, Arcadia, Ecl. XI:

Ai, ai, seccan le spine, et poi che un poco
Son state ad ricoprar l'antica forza,
Ciascuna torna, e nasce al proprio loco;
Ma noi, poi che una volta il ciel ne sforza,
Vento, nè sol, nè pioggia, o primavera
Basta ad tornarne in la terrena scorza.[13]

Alamanni, Ecl. II, also paraphrases Moschus:

Le liete rose, le fresche herbe e verdi,
Le violette, i fior vermigli e' i persi
Bene han la vita lor caduca e frale,
Ma' l'aure dolci, i sol benigni e l'acque
Rendon gli spirti lor che d'anno in anno
Tornan piu che mai belli al nuovo aprile,
Ma (lassi) non virtù, regni, o thesoro
À noi render porrian quest' alma luce;

[13] Professor Mustard kindly calls my attention to a passage of Castiglione's Alcon, "which will remind the English reader of the splendid passage in Lycidas about the Day-star and the ocean bed":

Vomeribus succisa suis moriuntur in arvis
Gramina: deinde iterum viridi de cespite surgunt:
Rupta semel non deinde annectunt stamina Parcae.
Aspice, decedens iam Sol declivis Olympo
Occidit, et moriens accendit sidera caelo;
Sed tamen occiduo cum laverit aequore currus,
Idem iterum terras orienti luce reviset:
Ast ubi nigra semel durae nos flumina mortis
Lavere, et clausa est immitis ianua regni,
Nulla umquam ad superos ducit via: lumina somnus
Urget perpetuus tenebrisque involvit amaris.
Tunc lacrimae incassum, tunc irrita vota precesque
Funduntur. fert vota Notus lacrimasque precesque.

and Tasso, Corinna:

> Cade il bianco ligustro, e poi risorge,
> E di nuovo germoglia;
> E dalle spine ancor purpurea rosa
> Còlta rinasce, e spiega
> L'odoroso suo grembo ai dolci raggi;
> Spargono i pini e i faggi
> Le frondi a terra, e di lor verde spoglia
> Poi rivestono i rami;
> Cade e risorge l'amorosa stella;
> Tu cadesti, Corinna (ahi duro caso!)
> Per non risorger mai.

Marot's treatment of the convention is briefer:

> D'où vient cela qu'on veoit l'herbe sechante
> Retourner vive, alors que l'esté vient,
> Et la personne au tumbeau trebuschane
> Tant grande soit, jamais plus ne revient?

And Spenser, November, improves on Marot:

> Whence is it, that the flouret of the field doth fade,
> And lyeth buryed long in Winters bale;
> Yet, soone as spring his mantle hath displayde,
> It floureth fresh, as it should never fayle?
> But thing on earth that is of most availe,
> As virtues braunch and beauties budde,
> Reliven not for any good.
> O heavie herse![14]

[14] This convention occurs also in the elegies of "A. W." and Francis Davison, published in Davison's *Poetical Rhapsody*, where it plays a great part. In Davison's Loss of Astraea's Favour, the contrast is drawn with most elaborate though graceful fulsomeness.

The most elaborate form of this commonplace is in Shelley's Adonais:

> Ah woe is me! Winter is come and gone,
>
> . . . .
>
> The airs and streams renew their joyous tone;
> The ants, the bees, the swallows reappear;
> Fresh leaves and flowers deck the dead Seasons' bier;
>
> . . . .
>
> Alas! that all we loved of him should be
> But for our grief, as if it had not been.

In Matthew Arnold's Thyrsis the convention is not so obvious:

> He hearkens not! light comer, he is flown!
>   What matters it? next year he will return,
>   And we shall have him in the sweet spring-days,
> With whitening hedges, and uncrumpling fern,
>   And blue-bells trembling by the forest-ways,
>   And scent of hay new-mown.
> But Thyrsis never more we swains shall see;
>   See him come back, and cut a smoother reed,
>   And blow a strain the world at last shall heed—
> For Time, not Corydon, hath conquer'd thee!

"Peace, Peace! He Is Not Dead"

If the pastoral dirge is mainly an expression of despair, it contains also an element of reassurance, of

---

The whole elegy is made up of eleven recurring forms of it. In the eclogue entitled Cuddy, ascribed to "A. W.," the contrast is drawn four times. William Drummond employs it in both his elegies.

consolation, in the thought that the dead is not really dead but lives on in another world. There is a hint of this in the dirges of Bion,[15] and Moschus,[16] though the convention as it recurs in the modern pastoral dates mainly from the fifth eclogue of Virgil. Here the elegy falls into two distinct songs by two shepherds: the first an expression of sorrow, the second of consolation, of gladness even; the first dwelling on Daphnis' death and the pity of it, the second, on his apotheosis; for Daphnis is not dead. He lives on in Olympus among the gods; nay, he is himself a god. This manner of treating the theme lent itself easily to imitation in the Christian pastoral, which regularly closes, as in a funeral service, with the thought of Heaven and the larger life. The transition from despair to reassurance is made either through the song of a second singer who bids the first cease his mournful strain and be comforted with happier thoughts,[17] or, when the dirge is one continuous song, through a sudden change of mood.[18]

[15] *Death of Adonis*, 97, λῆγε γόων κυθέρεια τὸ σήμερον, ἴσχεο κομμῶν. This with Theocritus' change of the refrain toward the end of his elegy to λήγετε βουκολικᾶς Μοῖσαι, ἴτε λήγετ' ἀοιδᾶς no doubt suggested such transitional lines as Spenser' "Cease now, my Muse, now cease thy sorrowes sourse."

[16] At the close of his lament, Moschus imagines his hero as continuing his song in Hades, and suggests that in reward for his sweet piping Persephone may send him back to his native hills—καὶ σὲ Βίων πέμψει τοῖς ὥρεσιν.

[17] For example, Ambrose Philips:

No more, mistaken Angelot, complain,
Albino lives, and all our tears are vain.

[18] Milton, Lycidas: "Weep no more woeful shepherds, weep no more."

The majority of modern pastoral elegies describe the blessedness of the dead in terms of classical religion and mythology, imitating and echoing Virgil closely,[19] or mix Pagan imagery with Christian theology in a curious confusion.[20] Sannazaro's Phyllis furnishes an illustration, which has the special interest of having influenced Milton: [21]

> At tu, sive altum felix colis aethera, seu iam
> Elysios inter manes coetusque verendos
> Lethaeos sequeris per stagna liquentia pisces,
>
> . . . .
>
> Adspice nos, mitisque veni; tu numen aquarum
> Semper eris, semper laetum piscantibus omen.

Of the more conventional use of this commonplace, perhaps the finest example is in Marot's elegy, the long passage beginning:

> Non, taisez vous c'est assez deploré:
> Elle est aux Champs Elisiens receue,

to which Spenser's vaunted paraphrase

> Why wayle we then? why weary we the Gods with playnts,
> As if some evill were to her betight?
> She raignes a goddesse now emong the saintes, etc.,[22]

[19] Tasso, for example, translates Virgil word for word. Pope and Ambrose Philips do little more.

[20] So Milton, Lycidas.

[21] So J. H. Hanford, *op. cit.*, 434.

[22] The consolation in Gay's travesty is less conventional:

> Thus wailed the louts in melancholy strain,
> Till bonny Susan sped across the plain,
> They seized the lass in apron clean arrayed
> And to the ale-house forced the willing maid;
> In ale and kisses they forget their cares,
> And Susan Blouzelinda's loss repairs.

is altogether inferior. Shelley's use of the convention is worth all the rest. He turns it freely into a magnificent expression of his Platonizing spirit. Calm philosophy succeeds to bitter despair:

> Peace, peace! he is not dead, he doth not sleep—
> He hath awakened from the dream of life—
> .   .   .   .
> He has outsoared the shadow of our night;
> Envy and calumny and hate and pain.
> And that unrest which men miscall delight,
> Can touch him not and torture not again;
> From the contagion of the world's slow stain
> He is secure, and now can never mourn
> A heart grown cold, a head grown gray in vain;
> Nor, when the spirit's self has ceased to burn,
> With sparkless ashes load an unlamented urn.
>
> He lives, he wakes—'tis Death is dead, not he;
> Morn not for Adonais.—Thou young Dawn,
> Turn all thy dew to splendour, for from thee
> The spirit thou lamentest is not gone;
> Ye caverns and ye forests, cease to moan!
> Cease, ye faint flowers and fountains, and thou Air,
> Which like a mourning veil thy scarf hadst thrown
> O'er the abandoned Earth, now leave it bare
> Even to the joyous stars which smile on its despair
>
> He is made one with Nature: there is heard
> His voice in all her music, from the moan
> Of thunder to the song of night's sweet bird;
> He is a presence to be felt and known

In darkness and in light, from herb and stone,
Spreading itself where'er that Power may move
Which has withdrawn his being to its own;
Which wields the world with never-wearied love,
Sustains it from beneath, and kindles it above.

In Matthew Arnold, as usual, the convention is less
obvious:

To a boon southern country he is fled,
    And now in happier air,
Wandering with the great Mother's train divine
    (And purer or more subtle soul than thee,
    I trow, the mighty Mother doth not see)
Within a folding of the Apennine,

Thou hearest the immortal chants of old!—
    Putting his sickle to the perilous grain
        In the hot cornfield of the Phrygian king,
For thee the Lityerses-song again
    Young Daphnis with his silver voice doth sing;
        Sings his Sicilian fold,
His sheep, his hapless love, his blinded eyes—
    And how a call celestial round him rang,
    And heavenward from the fountain-brink he sprang,
And all the marvel of the golden skies.

THE PRISON OF THE PRESENT

Many will recall Gilbert Murray's notable address on the *Religion of a Man of Letters*. "The greater part of life," he said, "is rigidly confined to the round of things that happen from hour to hour. It is exposed for circumstances to beat upon; its stream of consciousness channeled and directed by events and environments of the moment. Man is imprisoned in the external present; and what we call a man's religion is to a great extent the thing that offers him a secret and permanent means of escape from this prison, a breaking of prison walls which leaves him standing, of course, in the present, but in a present so enlarged and enfranchised that it is become not a prison but a free world. Religion in its narrowest sense is always seeking for *soteria*, for escape, for some salvation from the terror to come, or deliverance from the body of this death."

That was some years ago, when we were in the thick of a desperate war. At that time we found escape from the anxieties, the discouragements, the terrors of the moment upon the wings of a high hope, a lofty vision of a "new heaven and a new earth." The very enormity of the conflict was less terrifying than inspiring. It seemed that the forces of good and of evil, which up to then had grappled through the centuries in inconclusive strife had now met in a final battle to the death. It seemed that the predatory instincts of mankind had at last become embodied and isolated in our definite enemies, and that all we had to do was to blast and shoot and starve them out of existence, and then rebuild the world on abiding foundations of peace and justice and goodwill. Beyond the wreck and wrack of war, through lurid smoke of guns and dust of crumbling walls, we glimpsed the promised land—or so we thought.

Now it appears that our dreamed-of promised land was but a paradise of fools. We have been defeated in our aspirations. The ideals for which we struggled seem to be evidenced only by the millions of little white crosses on the graves of the dead. We, the living, are back in the same old world—yet not the same. Hope and faith and resolution have for the time largely departed from it. Some of us are living furiously, recklessly in the present; "getting and spending, we lay waste our lives" within the narrow confines of to-day, utterly heedless of to-morrow— after us the deluge! others, retaining still some sense of social responsibility, but cheated of our high faith in human nature, despair of the future of our civilization; and all of us, in greater or less degree, have lost our vision of the promised land, and are beating ineffectually against our prison walls, "seeking some salvation from the terror to come or deliverance from the body of this death."

It should take courage to propose another remedy for a sick and weary world. Yet one might make bold to say, even in a generation to whom yesterday's newspaper is a tale that is told and forgotten, that we are suffering most of all from *presentitis;* that there may be found a bracing tonic in a change of scene; and that the religion of the man of letters proffers us a saving grace. By man of letters we do not mean the scholar in the narrow sense, the specialist, the technician in letters, but such a man as we all, no matter what may be our occupations or professions, have it in us to become—I mean, the humanist who has read and pondered and entered sympathetically into the precious records of our great human story. He may or he may not have received the baptism of the Holy Ghost, but something akin to it has entered into and possessed his soul; the human spirit, the divinely patient and unconquerable spirit of man, the spirit of going on, of climbing up and glimpsing the promised land.

But the way is long and hard; there are many halts and now and then a retreat; and the man of letters is not swept from the ground by impossible hope; neither is he cast down by vain despair. He knows that no people, whether in victory or in defeat, have ever stepped out of a great war into the promised land. He remembers that after the war for independence in this country the peace which was signed by the United States of America was followed by a period of disunion, of flying apart, of incapacity for concerted action, of local jealousies and animosities, of insurrections within the states and threats of open war between them—five years of dreary drifting toward anarchy, until out of the desperate necessities of the situation there was wrought, as by a miracle, the Constitution of these States.

He remembers also that our Civil War was a war of high and generous ideals. Julia Ward Howe set the armies of liberation marching to sublime words which became the Nation's battle hymn:

In the beauty of the lilies Christ was born across the sea
With a glory in his bosom that transfigures you and me.
As he died to make men holy, let us die to make men free;
Our God is marching on.

And Abraham Lincoln towered far above all sordid and violent passions of his time, pleading for charity for all and malice toward none, praying confidently that out of the shedding of blood there should come "under God a new birth of freedom." And there came instead a period of bitter reaction, a period, one might almost say, of charity toward none and malice toward all—the tragic spectacle of the murder of the noblest citizen of this Republic; of the impeachment trial of Andrew Johnson, the angry passions of the multitude demanding a human sacrifice; of so-called reconstruction: in the south, the Carpet Baggers and the Ku Klux Klan; in the north, the scandals of the Crédit Mobilier and of the notorious Tweed Ring. For a time, a long wearisome time, it seemed as if the "new birth of freedom" had perished with him who had uttered the Nation's high resolve.

·The man of letters recalls also the long war which ended on the field of Waterloo in 1815, singularly like the World War of our day in that it engaged all the important peoples of Europe and that it was complicated with a widespread fear of the extreme ideas of Revolutionary France, which threatened the downfall of the established order everywhere. Like our war, it was a war to end all wars and usher in the golden age. In England, especially, the people hailed the peace with joyous relief. "O wondrous peace," they cried, O peace without a parallel! Yet this wondrous peace was followed by a gloomy period of disintegration, of class divisions and conflicts, of gross materialism, of incapacity for going forward, beside which the reaction of our time is but the shadow of a shadow.

There is nothing unique in our present situation. All great wars which tax the energies and resources of a people to the utmost induce an extreme intoxication of the passions of fear and of hope, a debauch of the emotions which is inevitably followed by the depressing morning after—a period of raw and jumpy nerves, of incapacity, of inertia, of despondent gloom, until the blood begins to course free and strong again, and the eyes grow clear to look the future resolutely in the face.

Our prison walls are built of our own blindness, and if we will but break the chains of our isolation in the storm and stress of the moment and escape into the larger, freer spaces of the centuries; if we will but seek a perspective which we can gain neither from romantic movies nor from the depressing chronicles of this morning's paper; if we will but resolve and make the effort to "see life steadily and see it whole," then we shall find in the present to a greater degree than in any like situation in the past ground for courage and for hope.

The courage to go on, strong in the faith that the promptings of our better nature are a sure guide to our feet and a lamp to our path, floods in upon us from brave moments of the past, when we break down the barriers which isolate our fragmentary lives. At the close of the Seven Years War, Robert Wood, then English Under-Secretary of State, took the preliminary articles of the Treaty of Paris to Lord Granville, President of the Council of Peace. Lord Granville was seriously ill; as it turned out, he had but a few days to live. Wood, seeing the critical condition he was in, proposed not to disturb him, but Lord Granville replied that it could not prolong his life to neglect his duty, and then quoted from the Iliad the words of Sarpedon to Glaucus: "Ah, friend, if once escaped from this battle, we were forever to be ageless and immortal, I would not myself fight in the foremost ranks, nor would I send thee into the war that giveth men renown: but now, since ten thousand fates of death beset us every way, and these no mortal may escape or avoid, now let us onward!" "He repeated the last phrase: 'Now let us onward!' several times," says Wood, "with a calm and determinate resignation, and then, after a pause, asked to have the treaty read." This is an example of how the tonic spirit of a race which faced life unflinchingly long ago may set a man on his feet again, marching to brave music.

Another example, less remote, I take from Drinkwater's *Lincoln:* the scene of the great crisis in the Cabinet when it was to be decided whether to evacuate Fort Sumter and so avoid the issue of war. Seward urges that war be averted by withdrawing the garrison, then nervously asks Lincoln: "Do you mind if I smoke?" Lincoln replies, "Not at all, not at all. My God, Seward, we need great courage, great faith!" Then, after a pause, Lincoln quotes: 'There is a tide in the affairs of men.' "Do you read Shakespeare, Seward?" Seward, smoking: "Shakespeare? No." Lincoln ejaculates, "Ah!" and decides to maintain the nation's honor.

I do not know whether this scene is authentic or fictitious. But it is essentially true. For Lincoln was, though not a scholar, a great humanist. "A great and powerful lover of mankind," his biographer called him, and to this fact we owe it that he stood throughout the storms of the Civil War, *saevis tranquillus in undis,* calm, unshaken in the midst of the raging sea.

It is isolation which makes cowards of us all. We know that in battle men will charge together with a cheer into the jaws of death where the chances are

that a single soldier would funk his duty. There is
nothing so disheartening, nothing so dispiriting, nothing which so inhibits brave and fruitful action as the
feeling of making a lone fight, and there is no greater
revelation which the religion of a man of letters can
give than that life is a march shoulder to shoulder
with a vast army of men and women who have kept the
faith and fought the good fight, they with us and we
with them, pressing

> On to the bound of the waste
> On to the City of God.

I am aware that I am urging a point of view which
seems exotic to the present generation. It is to us
almost a religion that the dead should bury their own
dead. We Americans, especially, are frantic wor-
shipers of the great god NOW! We rebel against
what we call the shackles of tradition; we feel cramped
in the garments which we think we have outgrown,
and we are keen to go our own way and live our own
lives without let or hindrance from the past. We assume that mere being on the go is progress and that
the fullness of life is to go whizzing, jazzing round and
round until we drop into our narrow graves at last.

We flatter ourselves overmuch; we are not of necessity progressive at all. "We stand upon the shoulders
of our ancestors and can see farther than they," said
John Bright, in a speech deprecating too much rev-
erence for the past. Yes, but we must first climb to

the shoulders of our ancestors before we can see farther than they. Biology, with its studies in heredity, reveals to us that the battles for civilization must be fought in the life of every individual, and that each generation must for itself catch step with the forward strides of the race. If the centuries have instilled in us an impulse to "struggle upward toward the light and let the ape and tiger die," nevertheless there is still strong in every one of us what the French call *la nostalgie pour la boue,* homesickness for the mud. If we could, as by a sponge, wipe out the checks, the restraints, nay, the inspirations of the past, we would be free, unhampered in our scramble for the mud.

We have not outgrown the teachings of Socrates and Plato; we have not outgrown the Sermon on the Mount. There are a thousand voices calling to us from the past, here warning us and restraining us, there bidding us onward, reviving us when we are spent and ever kindling afresh the divine flame. We cannot afford to stop our ears to them. There are a thousand battlefields of the past where men have fought and died that we "might have life and have it more abundantly." We cannot afford to be ignorant of them. There are a thousand noble spirits who have dragged themselves from the mud, climbed the heights, and caught the larger view. We cannot afford to forego their companionship. We cannot afford to lose the treasures of the human spirit. "Is not life more than meat and the body more than raiment?" It is the first business of the home, of the church, and of the school to keep civilization alive.

And civilization is a plant which requires tender and thoughtful nurture. It does not consist alone, as many think, in Ford factories and aeroplanes and high explosives. It does not consist alone in that machine efficiency whose dehumanizing monotony the French dramatist, Brieux, has vividly pictured in his *Americains Chez Nous.* "Your economy of movements and maximum of production, your Taylorism, as you call it," says one of his characters; "if you want my opinion, I call it terrorism. Over and over again the same motions, over and over again, over and over again—*toujours, toujours, toujours!* I declare it is enough to make one mad."

Well, we must have efficiency. We must have more, not less of scientific education; more, not less of applied science; more, not less of dominion over nature; more, not less of power. But if that power is not to be turned to our destruction; if it is to be employed to enrich human life and raise the level of human wellbeing, then there must be not less but more of human sympathy—more of the faith in man which comes of "seeing life steadily and seeing it whole," more of the courage which comes of the reassuring touch of shoulder to shoulder—a deeper and larger humanism,—and now more than ever in the history of this stumbling, struggling, inspiring world "the proper study of mankind is Man."

JOHN BRIGHT

In 1815, the Battle of Waterloo brought to an end the long wars which England had waged first against revolutionary France and later against the Empire of Napoleon; and the people gasped in their exhaustion, "O Wondrous Peace, O Peace without a Parallel!"

This double deliverance was, however, bought at a great price. England before the French Revolution was the most liberal country in Europe, and viewed the moderate beginnings of that Revolution with benevolent neutrality. James Fox hailed the Fall of the Bastile as "How much the greatest event that has happened in the world, and how much the best!" and many felt as he did. That was in 1789. In 1793, the execution of Louis XVI and, following upon that, the Reign of Terror produced a violent reaction. Fox kept his head and maintained that, in spite of the excesses which are its birth pangs, "liberty is order, liberty is strength," but he stood almost alone. The great majority of Englishmen were not only shocked, but utterly panic-stricken in the face of the world crusade for "liberty, equality and fraternity"; they trembled for the safety of their own established order, of the Government, of the Church, of property itself; and Pitt was driven to war. While their soldiers were fighting republicanism on the Continent, an army of spies was hunting down political heresies at home. It was dangerous for liberalism to raise its head. To criticise the Government, to attack corruption, to say a word against any institution of church or state, to raise a voice for reform, was to be persecuted, probably to be arrested as a Jacobin and thrown into prison. The habeas corpus act was honored more in the breach than in the observance; aliens were deported with little ceremony; every form of repression was practised in the name of patriotism; and, worst of all, the mind of the governing class, which up to 1793 was being gradually warmed into sympathetic concern for the people, was now congealed and hardened by a paralyzing fear of making any concession to popular claims.

Then came the threat of Napoleonic domination; and when this spectre, too, was put away, England was left in a state of physical and spiritual bankruptcy at the very moment when the problems of peace demanded all the sane and intelligent resources of the Nation. For, while reactionary politicians were making desperate efforts to stand still or even go back, the world persisted in moving on. Economic forces were working under their very noses a revolution of which they were only vaguely yet resentfully aware.

"Let trade and commerce, laws and learning die," cried
    one,
But leave us still our old nobility."

The small farms and village commons had already been largely swallowed up in the great estates, and the division was clearly drawn between a landed aristocracy and a tenant class. Steam and iron were conspiring to press manufacturing forward to a first place in the nation's business. In the north, especially, great factory towns were springing up—great blotches in a smiling land. The quaint and pleasant villages of an earlier day were giving place to chimneys belching smoke and soot; and there was beginning to come about both in agriculture and in industry that geographical and sentimental divorce between the employing class and the wage-earning class which has raised the tremendous and, up to the present moment, the baffling problem of our modern world.

Meantime the Country was ruled by a mad king and a profligate prince; and Parliament was an oligarchy of the great lords of the land who were hand in glove with a firmly intrenched Established Church. It must be said for this ruling class that they were, generally speaking, a jovial, honorable, sportsman crew, ready to fight at the drop of the hat for the glory of old England. But the glory of England was to them the glory of their class; and they were equally disposed to maintain that against enemies abroad and the rabble at home.

Perhaps the most notorious instance of class legislation of the time was the Corn Laws of 1815, the first measure of reconstruction after the great wars. These laws placed prohibitive import duties upon the essential foodstuffs of the country, raising the price of bread, flagrantly robbing Peter to pay Paul, and causing incalculable distress to the poor. This called forth the bitter lines of Lord Byron:

> For what were all these landed patriots born?
> To hunt and vote, and raise the price of corn.

The working class, indeed the people in general, had no voice in the government. They were thought to be too ignorant to be entrusted with the franchise. Probably three-fourths of them could neither read nor write, so removed were they from the means of education. But they were human beings, many in distress. They had lost confidence in their masters; and having felt the ferment of new ideas, were groping blindly toward popular sovereignty. Theoretically, at any rate, they possessed the rights of free assembly and petition, and through means like these they began to assert themselves. For example, in August, 1819, a great meeting was called in St. Peter's Field at Manchester to make a demonstration for the reform of Parliament and the suffrage. On the appointed day men came marching into Manchester by thousands from the surrounding country, waving banners with such revolutionary slogans as: "No Corn Laws"; "Annual Parliaments"; "Universal Suffrage"; "Vote by Ballot."

The magistrates became alarmed. They collected such police as were available and a band of volunteer soldiers, and ordered them to charge the mob and arrest the speakers. In an instant there was terrible confusion. People were trampled underfoot; some were thus killed; some were sabered to death; and three or four hundred were more or less severely injured. Hunt, the principal speaker, and his associates were arrested and sentenced to prison on a charge of "conspiracy to alter the legal frame of government and the constitution of these realms by force and threats, and with meeting tumultuously at Manchester." This was the celebrated Peterloo massacre.

The government sustained the magistrates, congratulated the soldiers, and later replied to the demonstration at Peterloo by the famous six acts restricting, among other liberties, the right of public assembly, and devising quicker means to deal with traitors.

Public opinion was, however, outraged at this violation of constitutional rights, and Shelley sent from Italy these flaming lines, which John Bright later quoted with great effect:

> Men of England, heirs of glory,
> Heroes of unwritten story,
> Nurslings of one mighty Mother,
> Hopes of her and one another;
> Rise like lions after slumber,
> In unvanquishable number.
> Shake your chains to earth like dew,
> Which in sleep has fallen on you.
> Ye are many—they are few.

When the Peterloo massacre occurred, John Bright was a boy of eight years. He was born at Rochdale, of an old Quaker family which had suffered not a little from religious persecution, and throughout his life Bright never ceased to protest against what he regarded as the unholy alliance of the English government with the Established Church. His father was a cotton manufacturer, and the son with his brothers fell heir to this business. He left school at the age of fifteen, and seems never to have thought of a university education, perhaps because the leading English universities were then closed to dissenters. Later in life, when he was installed as Rector of the University of Glasgow, he made a public address in which he lamented this handicap; but neither in his clear grasp of public questions nor in the simple and forceful eloquence of his spoken and written words does Bright ever betray the lack of what we call education. His sympathetic heart, his passion for humanity, impelled him more than any academic requirements could have done to read, to ponder, to master our great human story. He found his greatest affinities in the Bible and in Milton, and from them he reinforced the native moral fervor which made him for almost fifty years the personification of the conscience of England. If he was not a great scholar, he was what is, perhaps, better, a great humanist, and this fact is the one key to his life and to his attitude toward every public question.

His earliest public activities were connected largely with the Rochdale Literary Society, which he founded at the age of twenty-two—a sort of people's forum which he frequently addressed. He remained a local figure until 1841, helping his brothers in the management of their prosperous business, making occasional addresses, mainly against church rates and the Corn Laws, and enjoying in a degree granted to few men the peace of a charming home and the companionship of a devoted wife.

Then fell the blow which seemed the end of all things, but proved the beginning of a larger, if more tumultuous career. Bright has told the story in his own words:

"At that time I was at Leamington, and on the day when Mr. Cobden called upon me—for he happened to be there at the time on a visit to some relatives—I was in the depths of grief, I might almost say of despair; for the light and the sunshine of my home had been extinguished. All that was left on earth of my young wife, except the memory of a sainted life, and a too brief happiness, was lying still and cold in the chamber above us. Mr. Cobden called upon me as his friend and addressed me, as you might suppose, with words of condolence. After a time he looked up and said, "There are thousands of houses in England at this moment where wives, mothers and children are dying of hunger. Now, when the first paroxysm of your grief is past, I would advise you to come with me and we will never rest until the Corn Law is repealed." I accepted his invitation. I knew that the description he had given of the homes of thousands was not an exaggerated description. I felt in my conscience that there was a work which somebody must do, and therefore I accepted his invitation, and from that time we never ceased to labor hard on behalf of the resolution which we had made. Now do not suppose that I wish you to imagine that he and I, when I say 'we,' were the only persons engaged in this great question. We were not even the first, though afterwards, perhaps, we became the foremost before the public—but there were others before us; and we were joined, not by scores but by hundreds and afterwards by thousands, and afterwards by countless multitudes; and afterwards famine itself, against which we had warred, joined us; and a great minister was converted, and **minorities became majorities, and finally the barrier** was entirely thrown down. And since then, though there has been suffering, and much suffering, in many homes in England, yet no wife and no mother and no child has been starved to death as the result of a famine made by law."

Bright here sums up in a paragraph a five-year campaign of incredible energy in which he and Richard Cobden went up and down the country, organizing, raising money, speaking from the stump, until an awakened public conscience together with a terrible famine in Ireland forced the repeal of the Corn Laws in 1846.

When he entered with Cobden upon this struggle, he broke with the traditions of his sect, which in his day enjoined a life of quiet aloofness from the conflicts of the world. He thought, however, that this break would be only temporary. But once in public life, it was not easy to retire; and when in 1843, Cobden and his friends constrained him to stand for Parliament, his strong reluctance to do so was only overcome by his sympathy for the helplessness of the masses and their great need of a friend and spokesman in the councils of the nation. So he stood for election, frankly avowing it to be his one ambition to be the representative and champion of the working class. "I am," he said in his public address to the electors, "a working man as well as you. My father was as poor as any man in this crowd. He was of your own body entirely. He boasts not—nor do I—of birth or of great family distinction. What he has made he has made by his own industry and successful commerce. What I have comes from him and from my own exertions. . . . I have no interest in seeking appointments under any government; I have no interest in pandering to the views of any government; I have nothing to gain by being the tool of any party. I come before you as the friend of my own class and order; as one of the people; as one who would on all occasions be the firm defender of your rights and the asserter of those privileges to which you are justly entitled. It is on these grounds that I offer myself to your notice; it is on these grounds that I solicit your suffrage."

Perhaps these words have a demagogic sound. They are, however, the very essence of sincerity.

During a stormy career of a quarter of a century in the House of Commons he was a free lance without party ties and without party support—a voice of the people crying in the wilderness. When, in 1868, Gladstone became the leader of the new Liberal Party, Bright's confidence in Gladstone was so great that he was persuaded to enter his cabinet. He did so, however, with a misgiving which he finely expressed in his own words. "I have not aspired at any time of my life . . . to the dignity of a Cabinet office. I should have preferred much to have remained in the common rank of simple citizenship in which hitherto I have lived. There is a passage in the Old Testament which has often struck me as being one of great beauty. Many of you will recollect that the prophet, in journeying to and fro, was very hospitably entertained by what is termed in the Bible a Shunammite woman. In return for her hospitality, he wished to make her some amends, and he called her to him and asked her what there was he should do for her. 'Shall I speak for thee to the king,' he asked, 'or to the captain of the host?' Now it has always appeared to me that the Shunammite woman returned a great answer. She replied, in declining the prophet's offer, 'I dwell among mine own people.' When the question was put to me whether I would step into the position in which I now find myself, the answer from my heart was the same—I wish to dwell among mine own people. Happily the time may have come—and I trust it has come—when in this country an honest man may enter the service of the crown and at the same time not feel it in any degree necessary to dissociate himself from his own people."

He was never quite happy in the Cabinet. The give and take, the compromise, of administrative responsibility was irksome to his direct and ardent temperament. He felt himself at the last, as at the first, the tribune of the people. He suffered with them in their struggles; he voiced their inarticulate wrongs; he drew his power from their innumerable strength. This was, I think, the source of his indomitable courage. His aloneness in the most august and the most unmerciful assembly in the world must have unnerved him had he not felt himself standing on the shoulders of the millions outside who were his people.

From the very first he had the attention of a hostile House. His maiden speech there was an almost incredible performance. One can imagine him as he arose and faced for the first time the great Sir Robert Peel and his colleagues at the head of the Government: a smallish man, but robust of frame, soberly but not too Quakerishly garbed; of strong, open countenance, a friendly soul flaming from keen, blue eyes; hardly a gesture, hardly a change of posture, accompanying a voice of marvelous reach and appeal —a voice now tender with tears, now thunderous with denunciation, but always, whether in pathos or humor or scorn, flowing from the wells of a kindly heart.

A first speech in Parliament—always a trying ordeal—is expected to be a sort of apology for one's existence. But John Bright did not apologize. He attacked Peel for the deliberate inaction of his government regarding the Corn Laws. He attacked Gladstone who had admitted that reform must come, but said that the time for it had not come. He struck and, as was his wont, he struck hard. "I am surprised," he said, "at the course pursued by the honorable baronet. (Sir Robert Peel.) I should be glad to see him, not the Minister of the Queen merely, but the minister of the people also. . . . He may have a laudable ambition—he may seek renown, but no man can be truly great who is content to serve an oligarchy who regard no interest but their own, and whose legislation proves that they have no sympathy with the wants of the great body of their countrymen. I live in the manufacturing districts; I am well acquainted with the wishes and feelings of the population; and I do not hesitate to say, when I view the disregard with which they are treated in this House, that the dangers which impend are greater than these which now surround us. I can assure the Right Honorable, the President of the Board of Trade (Gladstone), that his flimsy excuses will not avail him at the bar of public opinion. He knows what is right and he refuses to do it; and whether the session be at the beginning or near its close, it is his duty to suggest measures of relief to the commerce of the country. That this is not the time is an excuse which is as untrue as it is insulting. When will the time come? Will monopoly resign its hold of the subsistence of the people? 'Can the Ethiopian change his skin, or the leopard his spots?' The Government knows what is right, the people demand it be done; and the Ministry who refuse to act incur an awful responsibility."

It is astonishing that such boldness of attack, which in another would have been resented as sheer bravado, should have commanded respectful, if unwilling, attention. Whenever Bright spoke, the House listened. His very audacity told upon his audience—a solitary voice, without party support, taking upon itself to be the scourge of ministries. More than that, a new tone had come into the oratory of Parliament—a religious tone, something of the moral earnestness and fire of the old prophets, insisting that righteousness and justice were the touchstones of public policy. But most important of all was the feeling that this curious and unique personality which had strangely come among them was the articulate voice of the masses of the people, who would not forever be denied by an inert and dilatory government.

A review of the public life of John Bright from 1843 to the end of his career would be a review of the history of England, and, in no small degree, of the history of the world, during this eventful period. Hardly a public question during this time is not touched and illuminated by his power to go directly to the heart of the subject. His activity in behalf of the repeal of the Corn Laws is no more important than his efforts for the extension of the franchise—for popular sovereignty—which bore fruit in the Reform Bill in 1867; or his part in the reform of the Church laws, which in England taxed a dissenting minority and in Ireland a mutinous majority of ten to one for the support of the Established Church; or his work for the betterment of the administration of Ireland—pleading for patience, for conciliation, for justice to a people made turbulent by centuries of oppression, at a time when English statesmen generally looked upon Ireland as revolution incarnate and saw no other remedy than that of putting on the screws.

In all this agitation, his broad tolerance, his human sympathy and his never failing appeal to the moral conscience, won him increasing respect and admiration. Then came the Crimean War, which placed him in opposition not to the government merely, not to Parliament merely, but to the passions of the multitude. It took a brave man to be an uncompromising reformer in an age of reaction; it took a braver man to be a pacifist in a country which by habit and almost by principle had come to look upon war as the chief business of a glorious empire.

It is now commonly agreed that the Crimean War was unnecessary. Indeed some historians regard it as nothing more than a criminal waste of men and treasure. It was at any rate a war which entailed horrible suffering in the armies who fought abroad as well as great distress among the poor at home. It committed England to the strange policy of alliance with the Turk—of energizing the "Sick Man of

Europe" that he might stand in the way of Russia. It was a war foisted upon the world by diplomats and kings. Yet it enlisted the support of the English people for two reasons. In the first place, it was fought to maintain the balance of power—that superstition which focused the fear and hatred of England upon any nation which, like Russia then, waxed too strong and prosperous and which must, therefore, be put out of the way. In the second place, although the war against Napoleon had been a "war to end all wars" —yet the "wondrous peace" of 1815 had ushered in an orgy of materialism, of industrial conflict, of sordid greed, which so sickened the hearts of the sensitive that even idealists turned with relief to war as the only knife which could cut out the canker of selfishness, and make whole the Nation.

"I wake," wrote the Poet-Laureate, "to the higher aims
Of a land that has lost for a little her lust of gold,
And love of a peace that was full of wrongs and shames,
Horrible, hateful, monstrous, not to be told;
And hail once more to the banner of battle unrolled.

      *   *   *   *   *

And many a darkness into the light shall leap
And shine in the sudden making of splendid names,
And noble thought be freer under the sun,
And the heart of a people beat with one desire."

But John Bright was not one of those who idealized war. "You have read," he said, "the tidings from the Crimea; you have perhaps shuddered at the slaughter;

you remember the terrific picture—I speak not of the battle, and the charge, and the tumultuous excitement of the conflict, but of the field after the battle. Russians in their frenzy or their terror, shooting Englishmen who would have offered them water to quench their agony of thirst; Englishmen in crowds, rifling the pockets of the men they had slain or wounded, taking their few shillings or roubles, and discovering among the plunder of the stiffening corpses images of the 'Virgin and the Child.' You have read this and your imagination has followed the fearful details. This is war—every crime which human nature can commit or imagine, every horror it can perpetrate or suffer; and this it is which our Christian Government recklessly plunges into, and which so many of your countrymen at this moment think it patriotic to applaud! You must excuse me if I cannot go with you —I will have no part in this terrible crime. My hands shall be unstained with the blood which is being shed. The necessity of maintaining themselves in office may influence an administration; delusions may mislead a people; . . . but no respect for men who form a government, no regard I have for going with the stream; and no fear of being deemed wanting in patriotism shall influence me in favor of a policy which, in my conscience, I believe to be as criminal before God as it is destructive of the true interest of my Country."

When, after John Bright's death, Gladstone spoke his eulogy in the House of Commons, he praised him most of all for his high courage in opposing a whole people bent on war. But at the time, he was ridiculed, execrated, burnt in effigy, and ostracized as a traitor. Yet he stood his ground amidst the tempest of abuse, never complaining, never blustering and never losing his poise. And never in his career did he appear to greater advantage and never did he attain a higher level of simple eloquence than when he arose in the House, faced Lord Palmerston, then the idol of a jingoistic people, and poured out his indignation upon a government which had so lightly entered upon a tragic and criminal war.

"It is very easy," he said at the close of his speech, "for the noble Lord (Palmerston) to rise and say that I am against war under all circumstances; and that if an enemy were to land on our shores, I make a calculation as to whether it would be cheaper to take him in or keep him out and that my opinion on this question is not to be considered either by Parliament or by the Country. I am not afraid of discussing the war with the noble Lord on his own principles. I understand the Blue Books as well as he; and, leaving out all fantastic and visionary notions about what will become of us if something is not done to destroy or cripple Russia, I say—and I say it with as much confidence as I ever said anything in my life—that the war cannot be justified out of these documents; and that impartial history will teach this to posterity if we do not comprehend it now. . . . Let it not be said that I am alone in my condemnation of this war, and of this incapable and guilty Administration. And even if I were alone, if mine were a solitary voice, raised amid the din of arms and the clamours of a venal press, I should have the consolation I have to-night— and which I trust will be mine to the last moment of my existence—the priceless consolation that no word of mine has tended to promote the squandering of my country's treasure or the spilling of one single drop of my country's blood."

A few years later, in 1861, the tables were curiously turned. The government which had perpetrated and prosecuted the Crimean War for the glory of England stood aghast at the enormity and barbarity of our Civil War, and was keen to mediate and stop the carnage; while John Bright, no longer a pacifist in the face of such an issue, gave himself heart and soul to the cause of the North. He saw at the outbreak of the conflict, what the English were slow to see, what we ourselves were slow to see, that the question at stake was only on the surface a political question, a constitutional question; that it was at bottom a moral question; that the fundamental issue was not whether the South should be free to set up an independent government, as the leading statesmen of England thought, but whether the South was to be free to perpetuate and propagate the bondage of a race of human beings. "I blame men," he said in a speech at Birmingham, "who are eager to admit into the family of Nations a State which offers itself to us, based on a principle . . . more odious and more blasphemous than was ever heretofore dreamed of in Christian or Pagan, in civilized or in savage times. The leader of this revolt proposes this monstrous thing—that over a territory forty times as large as England, the blight and curse of slavery should be forever perpetuated. I cannot believe, for my part, that such a fate will befall that fair land, stricken though it now is with the ravages of war. . . . I have another and a far brighter vision before my gaze. It may be but a vision but I will cherish it. I see one vast confederation stretching from the frozen North in unbroken line to the glowing South and from the wild billows of the Atlantic westward to the calmer waters of the Pacific Main,—and I see one people, and one language, and one law, and one faith, and over all that wide continent, the home of freedom, and a refuge for the oppressed of every land and clime."

That interesting book, *The Education of Henry Adams,* is nowhere more interesting than in the picture which it draws of the state of opinion in England of this crucial period—the seemingly willful misunderstanding, the crass prejudice, at best the indifference, of a large part of the population with regard to the Union. Devotees of the balance-of-power principle welcomed the prospect of the dismemberment of the young giant in the West. Liberals, like Sir John Russell, took the view that the North was contending for empire, the South for independence. Even Gladstone favored the recognition of the Southern Confederacy. But the mass of the people, the working classes were with the North; and—what is most remarkable— those to whom the war brought personal calamity, the cotton workers, thrown out of employment and in dire distress, because no cotton came through the blockade by the North of the Southern ports,—these workers preferred to starve rather than prejudice the cause which John Bright showed them to be the cause of freedom. Never in his life did John Bright strike harder blows in any cause, and Henry Adams calls him the hardest hitter in England.

Perhaps the greatest speech made by Bright in the cause of the Union was the speech at Rochdale, Christmas, 1861, at the most critical moment of the war. Mason and Slidell had been sent by Jefferson Davis on the British ship, "Trent," to arouse England and France to war against the North. On the eighth of November the ship was stopped on its voyage by Captain Wilkes, and Mason and Slidell were seized and made prisoners. This violation of international law stirred up tremendous feeling. It was not now a question only of the recognition of the Southern Confederacy, it was a question of war with the North. No one can measure how disastrous it would have been for us and for the world, had either course been taken; and therefore no one can measure what a friend in this dark hour we had in John Bright. Much of the speech at Rochdale is, perhaps, mainly of historical interest: his attack upon the belligerency of the British Government; his plea for patience, for peaceable adjustment; his exhortation not to hamper, not to dishearten, not to cripple a great cause. Heard and read in the light of the time, in their setting of prejudice, of passion, of impending doom, his words inspired in the friends of America the most profound gratitude—our historian Motley read them and thanked God for John Bright— words which now in the light of other days and other concerns we can read with indifferent calm. But there is one passage of that speech which is not touched with age; which still has potency to stir at least those who feel that, whatever the mistakes of this Republic or of Great Britain in the past and now, the well-being of the world—the cause of freedom everywhere—is not promoted by the makers of discord between the two greatest powers of the English speaking race.

"At this very moment," he said at Rochdale, "there are millions in the United States who personally or whose immediate parents, have at one time been citizens of this Country. They found a home in the far West; they subdued the wilderness; they met with plenty there, which was not offered them in their native country; and they have become a great people. There may be persons in England who are jealous of the States; there may be men who dislike democracy, and who hate a republic; there may be those whose sympathies warm toward the slave oligarchy of the South; but of this I am certain, that only misrepresentation the most gross or calumny the most wicked can sever the tie which unites the great mass of the people of this country with their friends and brethren beyond the Atlantic.

"Now whether the Union will be restored or not, or the South achieve an unhonoured independence or not,

I know not and I predict not. But this I think I know —that in a few years, a very few years, the twenty millions of freemen in the North will be thirty millions or even fifty millions—a population equal or exceeding that of this kingdom. When that time comes, I pray that it may not be said amongst them that in the darkest hour of their Country's trials, England, the land of their fathers, looked on with icy coldness and saw unmoved the perils and calamities of their children. As for me, I have but this to say: I am but one in this audience, and but one in the citizenship of this Country; if all other tongues are silent, mine shall speak for that policy which gives hope to the bondsmen of the South, and which tends to generous thoughts and generous deeds between the two great nations who speak the English language, and from their origin are alike entitled to the English name."

At the close of the war, in 1865, he turned this plea into a great prophecy: "I believe that in the centuries which are to come it will be the greatest pride and the highest renown of England that from her loins have sprung a hundred million—it may be two hundred million—of men who dwell and prosper on that continent which the old Genoese gave to Europe. Sir, if the sentiments which I have uttered shall become the sentiments of the Parliament and the people of the United Kingdom—if the moderation which I have described shall mark the course of the Government and of the people of the United States—then, notwithstanding some present irritations and some present distrust

—and I have faith both in us and in them—I believe that these two great Commonwealths will march abreast, the parents and guardians of freedom and justice, wheresoever their language shall be spoken and their power extend."

ANTICIPATIONS OF THE DOCTRINE OF EVOLUTION AMONG THE GREEKS

"To one small people," said Henry Sumner Maine, "it was given to institute the principle of progress. That people was the Greek. Except the blind forces of Nature, nothing moves in this world which is not Greek in its origin."

This is a rather startling way of saying that all the roads of our intellectual life lead, albeit with many detours, back to Greece. Even so, we cannot but question whether the generalization is not too broad—whether it is not an overstatement of the truth. Science, for example, we commonly think of as a modern growth, without roots in the past; and as for evolution, this idea is popularly supposed to have sprung directly, "full-panoplied," from the brain of Charles Darwin, like Athena from the head of Zeus.

In a sense, the popular notion is, of course, not far wrong. The scientific habit of building hypotheses upon the data of experience and observation—the inductive method—is more modern than ancient, and Darwin was the first to place the evolutionary theory upon a scientific basis.

In fact, however, the doctrine of evolution is not a single idea, but a cluster of ideas born at different times and in different minds. The early philosophers of Greece conceived the theory in its broad outlines, and their speculations in this field influenced the nature philosophy of the eighteenth and the early nineteenth centuries. Evolution was already in the air when Darwin began his work, and gave direction to his research. He, like any other great thinker, was not only the father of a new trend of thought, but the intellectual child of his time. It would be rash, therefore, to assert that our evolutionary point of view goes back directly to Greece, but it would be equally rash to say that our thinking on this subject has no relation to the thinking of the Greeks.

The first fact that we have to note with regard to the early Greek philosophers is that they concerned themselves very largely with the explanation of the external world, its origin, its development, its phenomena, and its destiny—an ambitious undertaking which, in the childhood of philosophy, they faced with a confident belief in the supreme efficacy of reason. With no scientific background and with no philosophical background save the fantasies of mythology, they left the gods out of the picture, and started to work out what they conceived to be a purely scientific view of things.

They began with the assumption of some fundamental element or elements. By the differentiation of this element or by a combination of elements, they tried to account for the origin of the complex forms of matter and life, usually by a single principle of change or motion.

They differed among themselves in many respects, but they all had in common a belief in the gradual development of more complex forms out of more simple and undifferentiated matter, and that this process of development is still going on and will continue to go on forever according to a definite ascertainable law. No room was left in their theories for divine interference or caprice, nor do we find anywhere among them the notion of special creation or creations, which is familiar to us from the cosmogony of the Book of Genesis. On the contrary, they all, without exception, hold to one idea—that of gradual change or evolution according to natural law. In Heraclitus, for instance, all existence is concerned as a flowing stream; it is always in a state of becoming.

There is not room in this paper to cover all hints or adumbrations of the evolutionary idea in Greek philosophy. It must suffice to call attention to the main anticipations of the doctrine. We may begin at once with Anaximander, the earliest philosopher about whose teaching we possess any considerable amount of information. He was born late in the seventh century, B.C. Our information about him is fragmentary, but there is enough to reconstruct the main outline of his theory of development.

He begins his cosmogony with the idea of a boundless mass of chaotic, undifferentiated matter. In this there starts a differentiating—probably a rotary motion—which tends to "separate out," to use his own phrase, that which is hot, dry, light and rare from that which is cold, heavy, moist and dense. The former tends to fly outward, the latter tends toward the center. By this process the cosmos takes form. In its beginning it is a vast globe with the densest matter forming a central kernel, the earth. Around this forms the next densest, the moist or watery element—a great enveloping ocean; outside of this envelope of water is a surrounding envelope of fire.

The action of the fire upon the water produces vapors, which, expanding, break up the outer husk of fire, scatters it in the forms of the heavenly bodies, and produces the atmosphere between the heavens and the earth-enveloping ocean. The action of the fiery bodies of the heaven continues to dry up the waters around the earth, until in places the water is all evaporated and dry land appears.

It is not necessary to go into further details of a cosmogony which, Haeckel says, marks Anaximander as the prophet of Laplace and Kant. Only enough of it is set forth to lead up to his biology, in which, again according to Haeckel, he is the prophet of Lamarck and Darwin.

It is important to note that in Anaximander's view, the earth was completely submerged by water in the early period. This is the prevailing idea among the philosophers—an inference drawn from two kinds of observations: the discovery of sea-fossils on the highest land, and the noticeable receding of the sea and ex-

tension of the land in places, within a single generation. From these phenomena, it was easy to infer that
at one time all the land was under water.

Terrestrial life could not, therefore, have existed in
the early period—an inference which led Anaximander
to an interesting biogenic conclusion: "The first creatures," he contends, "were produced in the moist element and were covered with prickly integuments. As
time went on they came out upon the drier part, and,
the integument soon breaking off, they changed their
manner of life."

We must examine this last statement carefully; for
on its interpretation must stand or fall Haeckel's view
that he was the prophet of Lamarck and Darwin. Some
—for example, Osborn in his interesting book, *From
the Greeks to Darwin* [1]—believe that Anaximander had
in mind a sudden transformation of marine into terrestrial life. He had, no doubt, observed, they think,
the birth of certain insects from water-larvæ, or the
transformation of the tadpole into the frog. The
change of which he speaks is, therefore, a chrysalis
change, not that of gradual adaptation of marine forms
to a land environment.

It is in this sense that Anaximander has been understood. DeMaillet, a writer on natural science early
in the eighteenth century, so understood him and so
passed the doctrine on. "All terrestrial animals," he

[1] From the gradual drying up of the moist element all living
creatures were produced, *beginning with men,* says Osborn. If
this is a correct interpretation of Anaximander, then Osborn's view
is correct; but I can find no authority for it.

says, "have their origin in marine forms by direct
descent; birds were derived from flying fishes, lions
from sea-lions, and man from the merman and the
mermaid." From his elaboration of the theme it is clear
that DeMaillet believed that this adaptation took place
in a very short time—enviable philosophy in which so
much thrilling experience is crowded into a single life!

It is not clear from the fragmentary records of Anaximander's philosophy that he must be interpreted in
this way. His problem was to account for the origin
of terrestrial life on the assumption that once there
was no land. Discarding the possibility of special
creation, and assuming that present forms of life are
implicit in nature from the beginning, he had but to
suppose that the earliest form of life was one which
could live in water. When in the course of time the
water was dried up and land appeared, some of these
marine forms adapted themselves to the changed conditions, "changing their manner of life."

Nothing but our reluctance to attribute modern
views to an ancient philosopher prevents our thinking
that Anaximander believed vaguely in the development
of one species from another. Man, he holds, is sprung
in the beginning from a different kind of living creature, since his ancestry must be found among the fishes.
But he gives another reason why man must be descended from another species—a reason which does
credit to a keen intellect: "Other animals," he points
out, "quickly shift for themselves, providing themselves with food. Man alone requires a long period

of suckling. Hence, had he been originally such as he is now, he could never have survived."

This is all we know about the biology or biogeny of Anaximander. It is, however, enough to show that he anticipated the principle that all life originates in water, *omne vivum ex aqua,* which is, I understand, an axiom of modern evolutionary science; that he had at least a vague notion that one species may arise from another; and that he was not blind to adaptation as necessary to survival.

The next philosopher who is of great interest in this connection is Empedocles, who lived a century after Anaximander. He had more to say about biology than the latter, but aside from a number of clever observations on embryology, sex in plants, and heredity, his ideas seem, for the most part, curious. He held, however, that the less differentiated forms of life were the first to arise, the more simple before the more complex; plants, for example, before animals. Animals came into being in the following way. Love— the cosmic power of attraction—working on the four elements, earth, air, fire, and water, combined them variously, producing separately hands, feet, heads, and the various organs of the body. These bodily parts wandered about seeking to unite with each other. Often the union was a monstrosity, but when suitable parts came together; in other words, when combinations occurred which were suited to their environment, they survived, while all misfits perished.

Grotesque as this appears to be, we have here the

important doctrine that imperfect forms of life are evolved only to perish, and that those forms which chance to be adapted to their environment survive. Osborn, therefore, gives Empedocles a very important place in the history of the evolutionary doctrine, calling him, indeed, the father of the theory of evolution.

That Empedocles made an impression on modern workers in this field is evident from a passage of Diderot, quoted by Osborn: "I may at least ask you, for example, who told you—you and Leibnitz and Clark and Newton—that in the first instances of the formation of animals some were not without heads and others were not without feet. I may mention that all faulty combinations of matter disappeared, and that those individuals only survived whose mechanism implied no important misadaptation and who had the power of supporting and perpetuating themselves."

In addition to the notion of favorable combinations as necessary to survival, Empedocles seems to have held also that of favorable variation as a factor in survival. Vertebration, he naïvely explained, was due to an invertebrate animal having tried to turn around too suddenly and broken its back in so doing! This variation was favorable and accordingly survived.

Contemporary with Empedocles, was Anaxagoras. In his view, all living things sprang originally from life sperms or seeds which were brought to earth in rain, and germinated in the moist places. In these "seeds" was the principle of intelligence ($\nu o\tilde{v}s$). Therefore all forms of life are akin; one kind is not "chopped from another," as he puts it. Plants breathe and have sensation, even intelligence; they are, indeed, animals fixed in the earth. The different grades of intelligence in animals and plants depend on the structure of the body. The intelligent principle is the same in all, but it has more opportunity for development in one body than in another. In other words, the degree of intelligence is conditioned on the degree of complexity in the bodily structure. In this connection we have a most interesting observation: "Man has surpassed other animals in intelligence because he had hands"— which recalls Franklin's characterization of Man as the tool-using animal, and also the great significance given in evolutionary thought to that "accidental variation" in a muscle which opposed the thumb to the fingers and so made a hand out of a paw and a man out of a beast.

The anticipation of this idea by Anaxagoras seems to have escaped Professor Osborn's attention, although he speaks at length on the significance of this variation in the evolution of man, and quotes from Erasmus Darwin's [2] poem on the *Temple of Nature,* in which a whole canto is given to the human hand:

> The hand, first gift of heaven! to man belongs;
> Untipped with claws, the circling fingers close,
> With rival points the bending thumbs oppose,
> Trace the nice lines of Form with sense refined,
> And clear ideas charm the thinking mind.

[2] Grandfather of Charles Darwin.

and the later parody:

> There was an ape in the days that were earlier;
> Centuries passed and his hair became curlier.
> Centuries more and his thumb gave a twist,
> And he was a Man and a Positivist.

There is no evidence that Anaxagoras taught the doctrine of the development of one species from another, but he did emphasize the kinship between all forms of life, and so approached the idea of a chain of life connecting all living things, which is clearly set forth by Aristotle.

In Aristotle, we have no longer the mere speculative philosopher. He built induction into a science. His whole life was one of patient and minute observation of the processes of nature. His works on the *Generation of Animals* and the *Natural History of Animals* show him to have been a careful student of Zoölogy in all its branches.

From his study of the analogies and resemblances between different species and his observations on the unity of type in certain classes of animals, he came to believe in a complete genetic life-series; that is to say, that the highest and most complex forms are lineally descended from the lowest and most simple, and that every species is a link in a chain which binds all together. Furthermore, in the development of one form into another, in the nice adjustment of parts in all, and in their adaptation to environment, he finds traces of purposeful design. Stripped of metaphysical terminology, his doctrine is that all Nature is a whole, and that there is in Nature an impulse towards perfection working towards an ever more perfect form or type. The lowest stage in the gradation of Nature is inorganic matter. Out of this by the progressive impulse springs the organic—plants, then plant-animals, or zoöphytes, as he calls them; then animals with feeling, sensibility, and power of locomotion; finally comes Man, the crowning product, in a degree the realization of Nature's aim and purpose—still imperfect but striving ceaselessly through Nature's urge towards perfection. Polyp and man—these are the lowest and highest rungs of Nature's ladder, between which in unbroken series are all the other existing species.

Paleontology had not yet shown the significance of extinct species and their relation to surviving forms, otherwise Aristotle would no doubt have been quick to give up his chain or ladder idea, as it has been called, for the branching tree theory of Lamarck and Darwin.

Aristotle's teleological idea of evolution prevailed until the time of Darwin. It is especially dominant in the philosophical thought of the eighteenth century. It kept alive the opposition to the special-creation dogma and the literal interpretation of the Genesis story in the Church. It inspired the theistic development theory of creation in Saint Augustine and Thomas Aquinas, and so prepared the way for the reconciliation of the evolutionary and the theological points of

view which has been effected in the minds of many
devout Churchmen, though not, it is manifest, in the
minds of all.[3]

[3] The most prominent even of the early Churchmen did not regard the Bible as a textbook on science. Osborn quotes in this
connection the sensible advice of Saint Augustine: "It very often
happens that there is some question as to the earth or the sky, or
the other elements of this world . . . respecting which one who
is not a Christian has knowledge derived from most certain reasoning or observation, and it is very disgraceful and mischievous
and of all things to be carefully avoided, that a Christian speaking
of such matters as being according to the Christian Scriptures, should
be heard by an unbeliever talking such nonsense that the unbeliever, perceiving him to be as wide of the mark as east from west,
can hardly restrain himself from laughing."

THAT OLD MAN ELOQUENT

At the age of ninety-seven, a year before his death, Isocrates published the *Panathenaicus*, one of the most ambitious of his discourses. He had been interrupted in the composition of it by a three years' illness, and it was only upon the urgency of his friends that he rose above his weakness and carried it through to completion.[1] It is not up to the level of his earlier work; his powers have manifestly declined; above all, the strong vanity of his artistic temperament,[2] whose frank expression elsewhere often offends the modern reader,[3] here falls into a senile querulousness as he sees the labors of his otherwise fortunate life failing of universal approval and acclaim.[4]

Yet the discourse is remarkable not so much for its senility as for its unflagging devotion to Athens. It is significant that the last discourse as well as the first great effort of his career, the *Panegyricus*, extols the noble history of the city of his fathers. Love of Athens is the one passion of his dispassionate nature; and second only to this is his love of Hellas. Or rather,

[1] *Panath.*, 267.
[2] Croiset *Hist. de la Litt. Grecque*, IV, p. 466, "Avec l'esprit d'un artiste, il en a le caracère," etc.
[3] The ancients were tolerant of self-laudation. See Hermogenes, Περὶ μεθόδου δεινότητος, 25.
[4] *Panath.*, 7.

both of these feelings are blended into a single passion
—a worship of Hellenism as a way of life, a saving religion [5] of which he conceives Athens to be the central
shrine [6] and himself a prophet commissioned by the
gods [7] to reconcile the quarrels of the Greeks and
unite them in a crusade against the barbarian world.
The course of events during the distressing period
of history through which he lived accorded badly with
his dreams. His own writings as well as those of his
contemporaries reflect the fatal incapacity of the Greek
city-state either to surrender any degree of its autonomy in the interest of a national unity or to leave inviolate the autonomy of other states. Athens, Sparta,
and Thebes, each in turn held for a time a place of
supremacy only to provoke by aggression general hatred and rebellion. The several states came to feel
more bitter against each other than against their common enemy, the Persian Empire, and did not scruple
to court the favor and use the aid of the "Great King"
in their selfish rivalries and wars.[8] Indeed the hope
of a united Hellas became more and more the shadow
of a shadow, until at last all Greece, exhausted and
demoralized by mutual warfare, submitted herself perforce to the leadership of Philip of Macedon.

Yet Isocrates never to the end of his life gave up
his purpose,[9] and it was doubtless this disinterested

<hr />

[5] Croiset, *op. cit.,* IV, p. 480, "Une image idéale de la grandeur
hellénique, une belle idole, à laquelle il rend un culte qui tient d
la religion et de la poésie."

[6] *Paneg.,* 50; *Antid.,* 295-299.

[7] *Philip,* 149.   [8] *Panath.,* 158-160.   [9] See *Letter,* III.

enthusiasm for a great cause, together with unusual
"health of body and soul" [10] and a degree of philosophical detachment from the heat and dust of conflict, which extended the span of his life over a century of extraordinary vicissitudes and disenchantments.

Much of the tradition regarding the life of Isocrates
must be received with caution. The formal biographies
of him which have come down to us are late compila-
tions [11] in which gossip is so confused with fact that
we can safely credit them only when their statements
are confirmed by his contemporaries or by Isocrates
himself.[12]

He was born in 436, five years before the beginning
of the Peloponnesian War, and died in 338, after the
battle of Chaeronea. He was one of five children—
four boys and one girl. Of his mother we know only
that her name was Heduto. His father, Theodorus,
carried on a business in the manufacture of flutes, and
was prosperous enough to perform expensive services
to the state and to give his children a good education.[13]
Isocrates says in the *Antidosis* that he himself had
such advantages in this regard as to give him greater
prominence among his fellow students than he later
enjoyed among his fellow citizens.[14]

---

[10] *Panath.*, 7.

[11] That of Dionysius of Halicarnassus prefixed to his essay on
Isocrates; that attributed to Plutarch in the *Lives of the Orators*;
that of Photius; the article on Isocrates in Suidas; and the
Anonymous Life, sometimes attributed to Zosimus.

[12] The *Antidosis*, the *Panathenaicus*, and the *Letters* are largely
autobiographical.

[13] See Jebb, *Attic Orators*, II, p. 3.

[14] *Antid.*, 161.

This little is all we know with certainty about his formal training. We have from his biographers the tradition that he profited not only by the established education of the Athenian youth of his time but also by the new learning which the sophists had introduced as a preparation for citizenship and practical success.[15] Indeed he is said to have gone to school to almost all of the professors of wisdom of his generation [16]—which can be true only in the sense that he made himself acquainted with all the intellectual forces which were stirring in his day and was stimulated by their influence.

He has, however, a rather clear relationship to two of the greatest teachers of this period. One of them was Gorgias of Leontini, the most renowned sophist of the rhetorical school, under whom it is likely that he was at one time a student.[17] Gorgias had visited Athens as a special ambassador from Leontini in 427, when Isocrates was a boy, and had then carried the Athenians off their feet by the brilliance of his oratory [18]—an oratory that was hardly prose but akin to poetry: rhythmical, ornate, and making its appeal not to the intellect alone but to the senses and the imagination as well. Later he spent some time in Athens

---

[15] The term sophist has not until later times any invidious associations. It was applied indiscriminately to all professors of the new learning—lecturers on literature, science, philosophy, and particularly oratory for which there was great demand in the democratic states.

[16] Jebb, Vol. II, p. 4.

[17] Blass, *Die Attische Beredsamkeit*, 2d ed., II, p. 14.

[18] Diodorus, XII, 15.

where his lectures were immensely popular.[19]   Next we hear of him as the orator at the Olympic Festival of 408 B. C., pleading with the assembled Greeks to reconcile their quarrels and unite in a war against the barbarians—which later becomes the theme of Isocrates' *Panegyricus* and the fixed idea of his life.   Afterward he settled down in Thessaly, where Isocrates is said to have heard his lectures.[20]

Isocrates was without doubt greatly influenced by Gorgias.   He probably owes to his teaching and example the idea which he later made peculiarly his own, namely, that the highest oratory should concern itself with broad, pan-Hellenic themes, and that the style of oratory should be as artistic as that of poetry and afford the same degree of pleasure.[21]

But when we attempt to estimate definitely what he took from Gorgias in the matter of style we are on uncertain ground.   The speeches of Gorgias, which startled his contemporaries, are lost, and we owe the fragments of them which we possess to the accident of their having been quoted to illustrate the extreme qualities of his style.   If we may judge by these alone, the oratory of Gorgias sought to depart as far as possible from the language of common speech: it was as artificial as poetry and even more bold in its diction, its imagery, its figures, and its constant effort to strike the grand note; in fact, Gorgias attempted to be a Pindar or an Aeschylus in prose.   His untamed rhetoric

---

[19] Plato, *Hippias Major*, 282 B.
[20] Cicero, *Or.*, 176.   [21] *Antid.*, 46, 47.

has its close analogue in the exuberant style of the
Elizabethan Age, particularly that manifestation of it
which is known as "Euphuism." [22] When Macbeth in
Shakespeare says, "Our monuments shall be the maws
of kites," he uses a daring phrase which might serve
as a translation of a fragment of Gorgias; [23] and when
Falstaff, primed with sack, harangues Prince Hal:
"Now I do not speak to thee in drink but in tears;
not in pleasure but in passion; not in words only but
in woes also," his parody of *Euphues* is quite in the
Gorgian manner, although it is, in fact, less extravagant
than Gorgias himself could be. What, for example,
could be more artificial than his "Shameful was your
sowing, baneful was your reaping," [24] in which we have
not only poetic metaphor, alliteration, and balanced
antithesis, but a close parallelism in sound—assonance
—which is rare even in poetry?

Now Isocrates did not attempt the grand manner,
and did, in fact, avoid the Gorgian excesses of style.[25]
He uses the Gorgian antitheses both of language and
of thought with better effect and with more concealing
artifice; and he employs alliteration and assonance
with greater continence.[26]   He abstains even to excess
from the language of metaphor, and he uses very seldom poetical or obsolete words or unusual compounds,

[22] This is pointed out by Gomperz, *Greek Thinkers*, I., p. 478.
[23] γῦπες ἔμψυχοι τάφοι.
[24] αἰσχρῶς μὲν ἔσπειρας, κακῶς δὲ ἐθέρισας.
[25] For the style of Isocrates, see Blass, *Die Attische Beredsamkeit*,
II, p. 130 ff; and Jebb, *Attic Orators*, II, p. 51.
[26] He is most Gorgian in his encomia (Blass, II, p. 130) but less
rhetorical in his later speeches.

confining himself rather to the words of current speech, using them with nice precision and combining them in a manner to produce an effect of dignity and of distinction. Blass quotes in illustration of this a sentence of the *Evagoras:* "He destroyed such numbers of the enemy in battle that many of the Persians, grieving for their own misfortunes, do not forget his valour," where the difference between the language of Isocrates and a bald statement that he killed many of the Persians is a difference, not of diction, but of imagination.

While Gorgias relies for his effect upon striking words and phrases, Isocrates subordinates the individual words and clauses to a larger unity. He is an architect, looking to the effect of the whole edifice, not that of single bricks or stones,[27] and taking infinite pains with composition—the smooth joining of part to part. He avoids studiously the clash of harsh consonants and all collocations of vowels at the end and the beginning of successive words—hiatus; and he has everywhere an ear sensitive to rhythms—not the exactly recurring rhythms of verse, but such as carry the voice buoyantly through the sentence upon wave after wave of sound without obtruding themselves upon the attention of the audience; for melody and rhythm are for Isocrates as important to artistic prose as to poetry.

The structural unit in Isocrates is the involved periodic sentence. This is extraordinarily long, sometimes occupying a page; often a half page; but it is so skillfully built that the parts in relation to each other and

[27] Demetrius, Περὶ ἑρμηνείας, 13.

to the whole are easily grasped; for Isocrates, no matter how often he balances clause against clause to round out his period, is always clear. The reader, however, even while marvelling at the architecture, is apt at times to weary of it, especially when Isocrates is so concerned about the symmetry of the sentence that he weakens the thought by padding, and, in straining for the effect of amplitude, becomes diffuse and tedious.

He is no less careful in the transitions from sentence to sentence and from division to division of the discourse; all is smooth and arranged according to plan. He does not dwell too long upon a single aspect of his subject lest he fatigue the mind. He opens with a sort of prelude which is not too closely pertinent to the theme, and digresses judiciously for the sake of variety. But all the parts of the discourse are rigorously subordinated to the design of an organic whole.[28]

Thus Isocrates took from Gorgias a style which was extremely artificial and made it artistic. In so doing, he fixed the form of rhetorical prose for the Greek world, and, through the influence of Cicero, for modern times as well.[29] And if the style of Gorgias lost something of its brilliance and its fire in being subdued by Isocrates to the restraints of art, perhaps the loss is compensated by the serenity and dignity of that eloquence which Dionysius urged all young orators to study who are ambitious to serve the state in a large

[28] The *Panathenaicus* is an exception.
[29] See Jebb, II, p. 68 ff.

way,[30] and which Bossuet singled out as a model for the oratory of the Church.[31]

The other teacher who left his impress upon Isocrates was the philosopher, Socrates. In the conversation at the close of Plato's *Phaedrus*, where Isocrates is mentioned as his "companion," [32] Socrates speaks with warm admiration of his brilliant qualities and prophesies a very distinguished future for him in the field of oratory, or in the field of philosophy should "some diviner impulse" lead him in that direction. The passage proves beyond question that there was at one time a close relationship between the young Isocrates and his teacher. Nor is there any reason to doubt that Isocrates cherished throughout his life a warm feeling for the philosopher.[33] The studied effort with which he echoes the striking features of Socrates' defense in his own *apologia pro vita sua*—the *Antidosis* —is evidence enough of his high regard.[34] Furthermore, certain characteristics of his life and work reflect the influence of Socrates: his aloofness from public life; [35] his critical attitude toward the excesses of

[30] *Critique on Isocrates*, 4.
[31] See Havet, Introduction to Cartelier's translation of the *Antidosis*, p. lxxxvi. For the "noble tone" of Isocrates, see Jebb, II, p. 42.
[32] ἑταῖρος
[33] The statement in Plutarch's *Life*, 839 F, that Isocrates grieved deeply over the death of Socrates and put on mourning for him is doubted, mainly on the ground of Isocrates' colorless reference to Socrates in *Busiris* 4. But his reference to Gorgias in *Antid.*, 155 ff., is also uncolored by any personal feeling.
[34] See *Antid.*, 21, 27, 33, 93, 95, 100, 145, 154, 179, 240, 321.
[35] In the *Antid.*, 150, he says that while he performed all the public services required of him by Athens, he held no office, shared no emolument, and abstained from the privileges of the courts, preferring a life of peace and tranquillity.

the Athenian democracy and his hatred of dema-
gogues; [36] his contempt for the sham pretensions of
some of the sophists; [37] his logical clearness and his
insistence on the proper definition of objectives and
terms; [38] his prejudice against the speculations of
philosophy on the origin of things as fruitless; [39] his
feeling that ideas are of value only as they can be
translated into action, and that education should be
practical and aim at right conduct in private and public
life; [40] his rationalism in religion combined with acquiescence in the forms of worship; [41] his emphasis upon
ethics and his earnest morality—now the prudential
morality of the Socrates of Xenophon, again the ideal-
istic morality of the Socrates of Plato,[42]—all these he
has in common with his master. If Gorgias intoxicated
him with the possibilities of style, Socrates was a sober-
ing influence and touched his life more deeply.

If we may rely upon the essential truth of the half
playful words attributed to Socrates in Plato's *Phaedrus*, two careers beckoned to one who possessed the
genius and the promise of Isocrates—that of the orator and that of the philosopher. Each, however, at
once attracted and repelled him. The one tended to
plunge him into the conflict of practical politics from

[36] See especially the *Areopagiticus* and the *Peace*.
[37] *Panath.*, 18; *Against the Sophists*, 3.
[38] *Peace*, 18; *Antid.*, 217; *Letter* VI, 7-9.
[39] *Antid.*, 261, 268.
[40] *Antid.*, 285.
[41] *Busiris*, 24-27; *To Nicocles*, 41.
[42] Compare *To Demonicus* and *To Nicocles* in general with
Nicocles, 49, 59; *Peace*, 31-34.

which his sensitive nature shrank; the other led logically into the realm of pure ideas to which his practical sense attached no value. In the end he attempted to be a philosopher and a statesman in one, avoiding what he regarded as the extremes of either. He endeavored to direct the affairs of Athens and of Greece without ever holding an office, and to mould public opinion without ever addressing a public assembly, by issuing from his study political pamphlets, or essays in rhetorical form, in which he set forth the proper conduct of the Greeks in the light of broad ideas.

The result of this dwelling on the "borderland between politics and philosophy" [43] was not altogether happy for Isocrates. In the *Panathenaicus,* we see a disappointed old man: he had been shut out from the fellowship of either camp; he had missed the zest of fighting, like Demosthenes, in the press of Athenian affairs, and he had been denied the consolation of retiring, like Plato, into a city of his dreams.

Isocrates usually gives as his excuse for remaining aloof from public life that he lacked the voice and the assurance which one had to possess in order to harangue the multitude and bandy words with the orators who haunt the rostrum.[44] But deeper than these physical handicaps, which he might perhaps have overcome, even as Demosthenes is said to have risen above

---

[43] μεθόρια φιλοσόφου τε ἀνδρὸς καὶ πολιτικοῦ, Plato, *Euthydemus,* 305 C. The nameless critic here described is undoubtedly Isocrates. See Thompson's essay on *The Philosophy of Isocrates and his Relation to the Socratic Schools,* in his edition of the *Phaedrus,* p. 181.

[44] *Phil.,* 81; *Panath.,* 10; *Letter I, 9; Letter VIII, 7.*

similar disabilities, lay the obstacle of his temperament
—his "love of peace and the quiet life." [45]

Two activities were therefore open to his retiring
nature, that of the writer and that of the teacher; and
since the former was not more lucrative then than it
commonly is to-day, there were reasons why he embraced them both. He tells us in the *Antidosis* that
he lost in the Peloponnesian War all the property which
his father had left to him, and that in order to repair
his fortune he took pupils for pay.[46]   In other words,
he embarked on the career of a sophist and opened a
school. This was probably in the year 392.[47]   Before
this, however, must be placed the decade in his life [48]
during which he wrote speeches for others to deliver
in the law courts.[49] We cannot easily set aside the
authority of Aristotle on this point and reject as spu-
rious the six forensic speeches which are included in
our manuscripts.[50]   And when Isocrates appears to
discredit this phase of his activity [15] and expresses
repeatedly his contempt for this kind of writing, we
must interpret his words to mean that he wishes this

[45] *Antid.*, 151.
[46] 161, 162.
[47] Jebb, II, p. 8.
[48] The first of the forensic speeches is dated 403; the last, 393.
See Jebb II, p. 7. Jebb accepts the tradition of Isocrates' school
in Chios and assigns it to the year 304; but this rests on the authority of a very careless statement of Plutarch, and is regarded as
dubious by Blass, II, p. 17.
[49] Every man was his own lawyer in the Athenian courts, and
when he did not feel competent to prepare his own plea he paid a
professional speech-writer, λογογράφος, to compose one for him.
[50] See Jebb II, pp. 7, 8.
[51] *Antid.*, 361.

episode in his work to be forgotten and that he dates his true career from the opening of his school.

Although Isocrates classes himself with the sophists, yet he sets himself sharply—and at times rancorously —apart from the other teachers of his age. He criticises his rivals and praises his own system mainly in two of his essays: that *Against the Sophists,* which he issued shortly after the opening of his school as an advertisement of his program; and the *Antidosis,* which he published near the end of his career, forty years later, as "an image of his life and work."

He denies a high place in education to teachers of the definite sciences such as geometry and astronomy, on the ground that these subjects have no relation to practical life and are of value only for mental discipline—"a gymnastic of the soul." [52] Students do well to spend some time on them, but only in order to train the mind for education of a greater and a more serious sort.[53] He attaches even less value to the speculative philosophers who concerned themselves with the nature of things; they disagree among themselves and prove the futility of searching for truth in such matters. Compare, for example, their contradictory views: "Anaxagoras maintained that the elements of being were infinite in number; Empedocles, that they were four; Ion, that they were three; Alcmaeon, that they were two; Parmenides, that they were one; and Gorgias, that there were none at all." [54] Such mental

---

[52] *Antid.,* 262-266.   [53] *Antid.,* 265.
[54] *Antid.,* 268, 269; cf. *Encomium on Helen,* 3.

legerdemain may have its place but it is barren of useful results, and no one should allow himself to be
stranded on these subtleties.[55]

Isocrates is more severe in his strictures on the professors of a debased form of dialectic which he calls
"eristic"—mere disputation.[56] They are impostors who
make impossible promises. They profess to be masters
of an absolute science of ethics and to be able to teach
their students for a price—and a ridiculously low price
at that—how to act rightly and be happy under all circumstances, whereas, in fact, our human nature is incapable of attaining to a science by which we can
anticipate all future contingencies and so order our
lives with prescience.[57] They pay no attention whatever to the practical virtues of private or of public life,
but are mere quibblers who by their captious reasoning
and sensational conclusions unsettle the minds of the
young and undermine their characters.[58] At the best
their teaching is useful only as sharpening the faculties
of their students.[59]

He condemns no less roundly the sophists of the
rhetorical school. They, like the eristics, are impostors
who bring all sophists into disrepute; [60] they promise
great things for a small price; [61] they pretend to aim
at the truth but strive for sensational effects, displaying

[55] *Antid.*, 208; *Panath.*, 26-28.
[56] Isocrates makes no distinction between dialectic and eristic, but
he refers under the latter term to such quibblers as are shown up
in Plato's *Euthydemus.* See Blass, II, p. 23.
[57] *Against the Sophists*, 1-3.
[58] *Helen*, 6-7.   [59] *Antid.*, 261.
[60] *Against the Sophists*, 11.   [61] *Against the Sophists*, 9.

their power in their epideictic oratory by speaking on mythical or paradoxical themes which have no relation to truth or to life.[62] They profess, moreover, that they can make a good speaker of any one; that the art of oratory is easily acquired by learning, largely from example, a number of elements or commonplaces which may be put together, like the letters of the alphabet, into speeches appropriate and effective for any occasion, whereas, in fact, oratory is not something which may be learned by rote from a master, but is a creative art which requires of the learner a vigorous and imaginative mind.[63] But the strongest objection to the professors of rhetoric is that they devote themselves mainly to the least reputable branch of oratory—the forensic. This is practical; but because it deals with petty controversies, not with large ideas, it is narrow; and because it aims neither at truth nor at justice, it is both false and immoral.[64]

As to his own system of education, Isocrates contents himself largely with a broad sketch of his ideas, dropping only hints here and there as to the content or the method of his instruction. He commends the traditional elementary education of Athenian youth [65] as a good gymnastic for the body and the mind. He admits also that exercise in other studies, such as eristic, is of value, if not carried too far, as a preparation for greater and more serious studies.[66]

---

[62] *Helen*, 8-13; *Panath.*, I.
[63] *Against the Sophists*, 12 ff.   [64] *Against the Sophists*, 12-20.
[65] *Panath.*, 26.   [66] *Panath.*, 26; *Antid.*, 265; *Letter V*, 3.

What, then, is the nature of his higher education? It consists, says Isocrates, in the cultivation of the art of discourse, ἡ τῶν λόγων παιδεία. This is a disappointing answer after we have listened to his diatribes on the inadequacy of other disciplines. We must, however, remind ourselves constantly in reading Isocrates that discourse, λόγος, is both the outward and the inward thought: it is not merely the form of expression, but reason, feeling and imagination as well; it is that by which we persuade others and by which we persuade ourselves; it is that by which we direct public affairs and by which we set our own house in order; it is in fine that endowment of our human nature which raises us above mere animality and enables us to live the civilized life.[67] The art of discourse may, therefore, be as broad as the whole life of civilized man; and this is just what Isocrates insisted that it should be. He complains that it had been limited in its scope—confined to quarrels in the courts,—and conceives it to be his business to deliver it from its narrow associations into the free atmosphere of great causes and large ideas. He himself chose, he says, to write discourses which were Hellenic in their breadth, dealing with the relations of states, and appropriate to be spoken at the pan-Hellenic assemblies; akin more to the literature which is composed in rhythm and set to music than to forensic oratory; setting forth facts in a style more imaginative and more ornate; employing thoughts which are more lofty and more novel; using figures of speech more

[67] *Antid.*, 253-255.

freely and more boldly; and giving the same measure
of pleasure as is afforded by poetry,—discourses which
are, moreover, further distinguished from the oratory
of the court room, which has to do with issues that
to-day are remembered and to-morrow forgotten, in
that they treat of subjects of permanent interest and
have, therefore, a value for all time.[68]

And it is oratory on this high plane, distinguished by
breadth of view and nobleness of tone, by literary
finish and charm, and by permanence of interest and
value, which he proposes to cultivate in his students.
They are to be led by their desire for praise and honor
not to suport causes which are unjust or petty but
those which are great and honorable, devoted to the
general good and the welfare of mankind; and the
effort which they make to write and speak on such
themes will tend to liberate their minds from mean
and selfish interests and ennoble their natures.[69]

Isocrates prides himself more upon the sound moral
influence of his work and teaching than upon any other
thing.   The primary object of his instruction is right
conduct in the man and in the citizen.[70]   Indeed there
are times when he seems to think of his influence as
expressing itself more worthily in action than in speech.
He says in the *Panathenaicus* that he took greater
pleasure in those of his students who were respected for
the character of their lives and deeds than in those who

[68] *Antid.*, 46 ff; cf. *Panath.*, 2, 136, 271.
[69] *Antid.*, 270 ff.
[70] *Antid.*, 284.

were reputed to be able speakers; [71] and it is significant
that the student in whom he took the greatest pride
was Timotheus, the general, to whom he pays a fine
tribute in the *Antidosis*.[72]

The "culture" which Isocrates professed to impart
was in one sense more narrow and in another, more
broad than the disciplines of other teachers. It was
more narrow in that he disparaged all knowledge, or
seeking after knowledge, which is not directly fruitful
in practical conduct. He attaches no value to the the-
oretical or speculative ethics of the teachers of disputation, who disagree among themselves. He himself is
content with a workable morality which is acknowledged by all men.[73] On the other hand, it was more
broad in that he thought of it as embracing all of the
relations of human existence. He criticises the professors of the sciences and of the arts in general because
they do not envisage the whole of life in their culture.
Outside of the narrow field of their specialties, they are
less cultivated than their students; they are often lacking in self-discipline; they are boorish in their private
relationships and contemptuous of the opinion of their
fellow-citizens. "Whom, then, do I call educated?" he
asks. "First, those who manage well the circumstances
which they encounter day by day, and who possess a
judgment which is accurate in meeting occasions as
they arise and rarely misses the expedient course of
action; next, those who are decent and honorable in

[71] *Panath.*, 87.   [72] 103 ff.   [73] *Antid.*, 84.

their intercourse with all with whom they associate, bearing easily and good-naturedly what is unpleasant or offensive in others and being themselves as agreeable and reasonable to their associates as it is humanly possible to be; furthermore, those who hold their pleasures always under control and are not unduly overcome by their misfortunes, bearing up under them bravely and in a manner worthy of our common nature; finally and most important of all, those who are not spoiled by successes and do not desert their true selves and become arrogant but hold their ground steadfastly as intelligent men, rejoicing no more in the good things which have come to them through chance than in those which through their own nature and intelligence are theirs from their birth. Those who have a character which is in accord not with one of these things but with all of them—these, I contend, are educated and complete men, possessed of all the virtues." [74]

In the *Antidosis*, Isocrates terms his culture a "philosophy" and himself a "philosopher." [75] He does not disclaim the title of sophist, but seems to prefer the other as more descriptive of his work. The appropriation of this term has been imputed to him for arrogance, as if he wished to set himself up as a Plato or an Aristotle. However, the word has at this time no definite association with speculative or abstract thought, signifying only a lover of wisdom or a seeker after the cultivated life,[76] and is in fact more general and modest

[74] *Panath.*, 28-32.   [75] 270.
[76] See Plato, *Phaedrus*, 278 D, and Thompson's note, for the history of the words, φιλόσοφος and σοφιστής.

than the honorable title of sophist which the sham pre-
tenders who called themselves sophists were only just
beginning to make invidious. Indeed, the use of this
term by Isocrates may be nothing more than a protest
against the preposterous claims made by certain sophists for the omnipotence of their instruction. He himself, at any rate, admits that formal training plays a
minor part in the making of a successful man: first and
most important, is native ability; next is practice or experience; and last is education; and no education
amounts to anything which does not involve hard work
on the part of the student himself.[77] Furthermore,
Isocrates, unlike the sophists whom he scorns, does not
claim for his discipline that it is a science which will
enable one to know exactly how to act in all the contingencies and crises of life. All that education can do is
to develop imaginative insight, sound opinion, power to
judge probabilities and to hit the right course of action
as each emergency arises. "For since it is not in the nature of man to attain a science by the possession of
which we can know positively what we should do or
what we should say, in the next resort I hold that man
to be wise who is able by his powers of conjecture to
arrive generally at the best course, and I hold that man
to be a philosopher who occupies himself with studies
from which he will most quickly gain that kind of
insight." [78]

[77] *Against the Sophists*, 14, 15; *Antid.*, 186-188.
[78] *Antid.*, 271; cf. 184; also *Panath.*, 28; *Against the Sophists*, 16;
Helen, 5.

The success of his school was very great. Notwithstanding that he charged a high tuition,[79] Isocrates boasts that he had more students than all the other sophists put together and that he amassed from his teaching a considerable fortune,[80] although he spent more on public services to Athens than upon his own household.[81]

His first students were Athenians; but after the publication of the *Panegyricus* in 380, his reputation spread gradually throughout Greece and attracted students from abroad. About this time, also, Athens rose to a position of power and influence as the head of the new naval confederacy, and was, furthermore, acknowledged to be the intellectual capital of the Greek world. "Athens," says Isocrates, "is looked upon as having become a school for the education of all able orators and teachers of oratory. And naturally so; for people observe that she holds forth the greatest prizes for those who have this ability and that she offers the greatest number and variety of fields of exercise to those who have chosen to enter contests of this character and want to train for them, and that, furthermore, everyone obtains here that practical experience which more than any other thing imparts ability to speak: and in addition to these advantages they consider that the catholicity and moderation of our speech, as well as our flexibility of mind and our love of letters, contribute in no small degree to the education of the orator." [82]

---

[79] He is said to have charged 1,000 drachmas for his course, Blass, II, p 22.   [80] *Antid.*, 39.   [81] *Antid.*, 158.
[82] *Antid.*, 295, cf. 299, and *Paneg.*, 50.

Isocrates, says Dionysius, was the most illustrious teacher of his time and made his school the "image of Athens." The ablest young men of Athens and of Hellas came to study under him, and went out from his school to become leaders in their various fields— oratory, history and statesmanship.[83] Among his students were the orators Isaeus, Lycurgus, and Hypereides; the historians Ephorus and Theopompus; the philosopher Speusippus; and the statesman and general Timotheus. And few, if any, of the literary men of his age, whether or not they were members of his school, were unaffected by his influence.[84]

Some of his students remained with him for three or four years, and seem to have retained for the master a strong feeling of affection as well as of high regard.[85] One of them, Timotheus, who exemplified in his life the doctrines of Isocrates,[86] set up a statue at Eleusis bearing this inscription: "Timotheus dedicates this statue of Isocrates to the goddesses of the temple, in token of his affection for the man and of his respect for his wisdom." [87]

Isocrates must have been throughout his life much occupied with his school. He was, however, given to hard work,[88] and found time and energy for a literary career. He called his writings orations, but they are

[83] *Critique on Isocrates, I*; cf, Cicero, de orat., 2, 94; Ecce tibi exortus est Isocrates . . . cuius e ludo tamquam ex equo Troiano meri principes exierunt. Cf. the similar claim made by Isocrates, himself, Letter IV, 2.

[84] Jebb, II, p. 13.

[85] *Antid.*, 87, 88.

[86] Blass, II, p. 52.

[87] [Plutarch], *Life*, 838 D.

[88] *Panath.*, 267.

such only in the sense that they are invested with the form and the atmosphere of oratory. He, himself, never delivered a speech, and few of his discourses were written for delivery.[89] He was in reality a political pamphleteer and has been called the first great publicist of all time. We must, however, guard against the implications of such modern terms. There was nothing about him of the facile journalist, nor was his writing ephemeral in its purpose or its character. He is said to have spent ten years in writing the *Panegyricus*—which is no doubt merely an exaggeration of the fact that he wrote slowly and with infinite pains. He believed that he was composing literature of permanent interest and value, and time has justified his faith.

It is in his political discourses that Isocrates finds the truest expression of himself, and it is upon them that he rests his fame—and rightly so. They are unquestionably distinguished among the political writings of his time for breadth of view and nobleness of tone. They transport the reader from the narrow circle of parochial existence into the generous atmosphere of a pan-Hellenic world; they are, as he says, Hellenic and deal in a large way with the relations of states. Even when he seeks to persuade Athens to a sound policy in her domestic affairs, he does so in the hope that she may be strong to help the weaker states and play an honorable and saving rôle in the affairs of Greece.[90]

[89] The forensic speeches and possibly the *Plaaicus*. See Jebb., II, p. 176.
[90] See Jebb, II, p. 41.

He is a loyal Athenian—no one can doubt his patriotism—but his sympathies embrace all Hellas. In his letter to the *Rulers of Mytilene* he says: "While my lack of voice and of assurance have kept me out of public speaking and active politics, I have, nevertheless, not been altogether useless nor unknown to fame; you will find that I have counseled and supported by my own efforts the orators who have been minded to speak for your good and for the good of other allies, and that I have myself composed more speeches in the cause of the freedom and autonomy of the Hellenes than all the ranters of the platform." [91]

"Freedom and Autonomy"—the catch words of Greek politics—are as precious to Isocrates as to any other. He differs from his contemporaries only in insisting upon "self-determination" as a sound principle of foreign policy for all the cities of Hellas. He takes the recognized law of Greek ethics, that power begets folly, folly begets insolence, and insolence begets ruin, and shows that it operates even more surely in the history of states than in the lives of individuals; [92] for a man may offend and die before paying the penalty, but states, which live forever, may not escape its workings.[93] Irresponsible power is like the bait of a trap: those who are lured by it are caught in its toils; [94] or it is like a courtesan: those who are enamored of it are destroyed in the end.[95] Imperialism has, in fact, been the curse of Athens, its only fruits being hatred, wars,

[91] *Letter VIII*, 7.   [92] *Areop.*, 4.
[93] *Peace*, 120.   [94] *Peace*, 343.   [95] *Peace*, 103.

and an empty treasury.[96] Sophrosuné, self-control—
the disposition to live and let live, to cherish freedom
for one's self and respect freedom in others—is the
saving virtue of states no less than of men in their relations to each other.[97] The Athenians and Spartans of
old, before the days of imperialism, practiced it and
made Hellas great. "They treated the Hellenes with
consideration and not with insolence, deeming it their
right to take command in the field but not to tyrannize
over them, desiring rather to be addressed as leaders
than as masters, and rather to be greeted as saviors
than to be reviled as destroyers; they won the Hellenic
cities to themselves by doing kindness instead of sub-
verting them by force, keeping their word more faith-
fully than men now keep their oaths, and considering
it to be their duty to abide by their covenants as by
the decrees of necessity; they exulted less in exercising
dominion than they gloried in living with self-control,
thinking it proper to feel toward the weaker as they
expected the stronger to feel toward themselves; and
while they regarded their home cities as their several
places of abode, yet they considered Hellas to be their
common fatherland." [98]

It was this spirit which Isocrates sought to call back
into the life of his generation as a means of putting an
end to the feuds which were tearing Hellas to pieces
and exhausting her vitality. He had no thought of
merging the individuality or the independence of the
Greek states in the sovereignty of a Greek empire, but

[96] *Peace,* 29.   [97] *Peace,* 28.   [98] *Paneg.,* 81.

had rather in mind the Delian League in its early days
before Athens had turned it into an empire maintained
by force; and what he dreamed of was a great confederacy of free states voluntarily united under a single
leadership, in the cause of a final and decisive war
against their common enemy, the Persian empire—"the
only war which is better than peace, being more like a
sacred mission than a military expedition." [99]

In advocating this crusade, he was not actuated alone
by racial prejudice. In a very celebrated passage of
the *Panegyricus,* he seems to conceive of Hellenism as
a brotherhood of culture, transcending the bounds of
race. "So far has Athens outdistanced the rest of mankind in thought and in speech that her pupils have become the teachers of the rest of the world; and she has
brought it about that the name 'Hellenes' is applied
rather to those who share our culture than to those who
share a common blood." [100]   If, then, he thinks of a
war of all Greeks against the barbarians as a sacred
duty, it is because he believes that civilization in order
to survive must be a militant force. Hellenism was an
outpost of culture, a lamp to be kept burning amid
the surrounding darkness; [101] and ever at the door of
Greece was Asia—sinister, threatening. "Isocrates saw
that the inevitable quarrel between Europe and Asia
which had existed from the "Trojan War" was the
great, abiding fact; he foresaw that it must soon come

[99] *Paneg.,* 182.
[100] 50.
[101] See the contrast between civilization and barbarism drawn in
the *Evagoras,* 47 ff.

to an issue, and throughout the later period of his life he was always watching for the inevitable day." [102]

The remarkable thing is not that Isocrates should have conceived this idea, but that in spite of rebuffs and discouragements he should have clung to it with such tenacity. Others had held it before him; Gorgias had made it the theme of his oration at the Olympic Festival in 408, and Lysias, in 384; moreover the shame of the "King's Peace" [103] was felt generally in Greece, and there was much irresponsible talk of a united campaign to deliver the Greeks in Europe from Persian interference and the Asiatic Greeks from Persian rule.[104] With Isocrates, however, it was something more than an idea; it was, as we have seen, a religious principle, to which he dedicated his unremitting zeal. "I might justly be praised by all," he says, "because throughout my whole life I have constantly employed such powers as I possess in warring on the barbarians, in condemning those who oppose my plan, and in striving to arouse to action whoever I think will best be able to benefit the Hellenes in any way or rob the barbarians of their prosperity." [105]

Two of his longer discourses are devoted entirely to this subject—the *Panegyricus*, published about 380, and the *Address to Philip*, about 346. To read them side by side apart from their historical setting is to be

[102] Bury, *History of Greece*, II, p. 301.
[103] The Peace of Antalcidas, 387 B.C., which had been dictated by the Persian King, surrendered the Greek cities on the Asiatic coast to Persian rule and conceded the right of the King to interfere in the relations of all Greek states.
[104] *Diodorus*, XV, 9, 19.   [105] *Phil.*, 130.

impressed by their disharmony. The *Panegyricus* draws a noble picture of Athens as the mother of civilization and of free institutions, and rests on this her claim to take the lead in a campaign against the barbarians.[106] The *Address to Philip* calls upon the King of Macedon, an absolute ruler of an uncultivated race, whom Demosthenes denounced as a barbarian and an enemy of Greece, to undertake what Isocrates now conceives that neither Athens nor any other Greek state can do; namely, to reconcile the quarrels of Greece and lead her against the common enemy.[107] Furthermore, the *Panegyricus* is an appeal to the minds of all Hellas. The name itself, which Isocrates chose, implies that he is following the tradition of Gorgias and Lysias by composing a speech suitable for a pan-Hellenic gathering. In the *Address to Philip* he has evidently lost confidence in such appeals. "Those who desire," he says, "to further some practical purpose and those who think that they have hit upon some plan for the common good must leave it to others to harangue at the public festivals, but must themselves win over some one to champion their cause from among men who are capable not only of speech but of action, and who occupy a high position in the world.[108] In other words, he rests his hope no longer on the collective wisdom of free com-

---

[106] In the *Panegyricus*, Isocrates seems at first to be thinking of a dual leadership—a concession to the fact that Sparta was then the first power in Greece, but his real purpose is to prove the right of Athens to the hegemony, as he himself states in the *Antidosis*, 57.

[107] *Philip*, 41.   [108] *Philip*, 13.

monwealths, but on a strong man, unfettered by constitutional limitations.[109]

This is a change in the point of view of Isocrates which has prejudiced his reputation in modern times.[110] He has been denounced as a traitor to Greece or pitied as a doddering old man.[111]   Even Havet, who in his admirable essay on Isocrates is most sympathetic, complains that the lofty tone which elsewhere permeates his writings is lacking in the *Address to Philip*.[112]

Perhaps the explanation of the change may be found in the thirty-four years of history which elapsed between the publication of the two discourses.   Not long after the *Panegyricus* was published, the views of Isocrates seem to have borne fruit in the organization of the new naval league under the leadership of Athens, in the year 378.[113]   This was a voluntary association of free states, and gave promise at the beginning of steering clear of the rocks of imperialism upon which the old confederacy of Delos had gone to pieces. "But," complains Isocrates, "Athens cared less for my advice than for the rantings of the platform orators;" [114] the same mistakes were made as in the old

---

[109] *Philip*, 14, 15.

[110] The criticism begins with Niebuhr: *Vorträge über alte Geschichte*, II, p. 73; whose abuse of Isocrates is so extreme as to be almost amusing.

[111] "Great and melancholy indeed is the change which has come over the old age of Isocrates"; Grote, *History of Greece*, XI, p. 436. Isocrates is now 90 years old.

[112] Introduction to Cartelier's Edition of the *Antidosis*, pp. XLV, LIX.

[113] Kessler: *Isokrates und die pan-hellenische Idee*, p. 24.

[114] *Phil.*, 129.

confederacy; and the bright promise of the league
ended in the wretched fiasco of the so-called Social
War (357-355)—a period of such demoralizing strife
that Isocrates prefers to it the shameful peace of
Antalcidas.[115]

This is a disconcerting period for lovers of democracy, and Isocrates' writings during this time, especially the *Peace*, the *Areopagiticus*, and the letter to
Archidamus, reveal the disenchantment which he himself experienced. He had been, unlike many of the in-
tellectuals of his age, a pronounced believer in democracy,[116] and as late as 359 he wrote in one of his letters [117] that "the life of a private man seemed to him
better than that of a king, and the honors of a free
state sweeter than those of a monarchy." But, while
he reaffirms his faith in a democratic ideal [118] even in
the discourses which belong to this period, it seems
clear that he considers the Athenian state, where he
complains, "insolence is regarded as democracy, law-
lessness as liberty, impudence of speech as equality,
and the license to do what one likes as happiness," [119] to be a caricature of what a democracy
should be.

At any rate, such a state was, in his mind, in no

---

[115] *Peace,* 16.
[116] See a very full discussion of this subject by Havet, *op. cit.,*
pp. xxvii ff and xl.
[117] VI.
[118] The democracy of Solon and Cleisthenes, in which a sovereign
people chose and submitted themselves to good leaders—an aristocracy in effect. *Areop.,* 20-27.
[119] *Areop.,* 20.

position to adopt and carry out any sound principle of foreign policy.[120] On the contrary, the Athenians were in this regard like freebooters, living from hand to mouth: now surfeited with plenty; now in extremity of want; [121] impoverished by war, yet conceiving war to be the only means of enriching themselves; [122] ready to listen to any demagogue who called them to arms,[123] no matter against whom,[124] yet unwilling themselves to train or make sacrifices for war, but hiring mercenaries to do their fighting for them, who turned out to be worse than brigands in the atrocities they perpetrated upon friends and foes alike.[125]

These are harsh words and unjust to Athens; [126] but even when full allowance is made for rhetorical exaggeration, they show at least that Isocrates had been disillusioned as to the powers of a pure democracy to manage a great military undertaking, and that it was not without good reason that he turned elsewhere to get support for his idea.[127]

It was in the midst of the Social War, about 356, that he wrote his letter to the young Archidamus, who

---

[120] *Areop.*, 12.
[121] *Peace*, 90.
[122] *Areop.*, 54.
[123] *Peace*, 6.
[124] *Peace*, 44.
[125] *Peace*, 44; *Letter to Archidamus*, 9, 10.
[126] Holm, in his history of this period, warns us against taking the pictures of Isocrates and Demosthenes of the degeneration of the Athenian democracy in the fourth century at their face value.
[127] For the general trend of opinion at this time in favor of monarchy, see Jebb, II, p. 21 ff., who emphasizes the fact that Isocrates and Aristotle were of one mind regarding Macedonian leadership.

was shortly to succeed his father, Agesilaus, on the throne of Sparta.[128] He pictures to him with very strong feeling the universal wretchedness of Greece, in which "no region can be found which is not rife with wars and factions and slaughters and evils untold"; and he calls upon Archidamus, who had apparently inherited his father's dream of carrying the war into Asia and setting Hellas free, to undertake this mission of deliverance.[129]

It is doubtful, however, whether this appeal was much more than the outpouring of a desperate mood to

---

[128] It is generally believed that Isocrates' first overture to any person in this matter was to Dionysius the elder, tyrant of Syracuse. See Jebb, II, p. 240, who says that Isocrates expressly states in his *Address to Philip,* 81, that he had made the same appeal to Dionysius. But all that Isocrates states here is that he is repeating to Philip the reasons which he had given to Dionysius for not taking part in public life. The fragment of the letter to Dionysius shows only that Isocrates appealed to him to perform "some service" for the good of Greece. It is extremely unlikely that he should have appealed to Dionysius, who was so occupied with his own problems in the far west, to head the expedition against Persia. The only definite evidence on this point is that of the 30th "Socratic Letter," attributed to Speusippus, which states that the discourse which Isocrates sent to Philip had been written first for Agesilaus, then revised slightly and "sold" to Dionysius, the tyrant of Syracuse, and finally had been revised still further and palmed off on Alexander of Thessaly. See Blass II, p. 89. If we are to treat this hopelessly inaccurate statement at all seriously, we must assume that it confuses Agesilaus with his son, Archidamus, and Alexander with Jason of Pherae whom Isocrates represents in his address to Philip as "talking of" an expedition against Persia, although there is no evidence whatever that Isocrates ever addressed a formal discourse to Jason on this subject. But if we substitute Archidamus for Agesilaus, then the Dionysius to whom, according to Speusippus, Isocrates next turned cannot be Dionysius the elder to whom the letter of Isocrates, of which we possess the introduction, was addressed; for he was dead long before Isocrates wrote to Archidamus. Obviously, the letter is worthless as evidence on this point.

[129] *Letter* IX, 8 ff.

a sympathetic friend, since Archidamus, before and after he succeeded to the kingship, found himself fully occupied with pressing affairs at home. It was with greater hope that, ten years later, Isocrates turned to Philip of Macedon as a man capable of carrying out so great an enterprise. Philip had announced his ambition to be a "captain-general of Hellas in a war against the Persians"; [130] he had by this time proved those qualities of leadership which made him one of the great figures of history; he had by his growing power induced Athens to conclude a ten years' state of war by the "Peace of Philocrates," and, shortly after the publication of Isocrates' address to him, he was elected a member of the Amphictyonic Council and given the presidency of the Pythian Games—a signal recognition of his paramount influence in Greek affairs. He was, in fact, the strongest man in Europe and commanded the greatest resources.[131]

It is clear that Isocrates had a great admiration for him. He believed that he was at heart friendly to Athens, and he had consistently urged Athens to cultivate friendly relations with him.[132] He regarded him as a pure Hellene of the line of Heracles,[133] as a man of education and culture,[134] and as a lover of Hellas with high ideals and broad vision [135]—a judgment in which

---

[130] Holm, Vol. III, p. 245; Hogarth, *Philip and Alexander of Macedon*, p. 97; *Diodorus*, XVI, 60.
[131] *Philip*, 137; 15.
[132] *Peace*, 22.
[133] *Philip*, 76; 32-34; 105.
[134] *Philip*, 29.
[135] *Philip*, 132.

Isocrates is supported by those historians whose views
of this period are not echoed from the orations of
Demosthenes.[136] Furthermore, he thought that Philip
was in a unique position to champion the cause of all
Hellas; other Greeks were too much identified with
their own states; they were restricted by local patriotism and by the bonds of local polities and laws:
"You," he says to Philip, "are privileged as one who is
above such limitations to consider all Hellas your
fatherland, as did the father of your race, and to be
ready to brave perils for her sake." [137]

It is true that the lofty tone of the *Panegyricus* is
absent from the *Address to Philip*. Isocrates had
dreamed that Athens, the author of Greek civilization,
should be the leader in its militant triumph; and he
could not with the same enthusiasm give to another the
place which he had reserved for her.[138] But he was giving up nothing more than his local sentiment and pride.
Philip was to be conceded the hegemony only; he was
to be the leader of a confederacy of free states. There
was not now in Isocrates' mind any more than when he
wrote the Panegyricus any thought of surrendering the
independence of Greek states to an imperial power.[139]

It turned out somewhat differently. Demosthenes
and the war party in Athens prevailed and forced the

[136] See Holm III, ch. 19; Bury II, ch. 6; Hogarth, *Philip and
Alexander of Macedon*.
[137] *Philip*, 127.
[138] See *Address to Philip*, 129.
[139] See Jebb, II, pp. 21 ff.

issue with Philip; the result was the battle of Chaeronea and the subjection by force of the Greek states to
the overlordship of the Macedonian king.[140]

Isocrates was no doubt oppressed by what he must
have regarded as the useless slaughter at Chaeronea.
But the tradition that he committed suicide on hearing
that Philip had won, made familiar through Milton's
lines:

> As that dishonest victory
> At Chaeronea, fatal to liberty,
> Killed with report that old man eloquent,[141]

is so improbable on the face of it and so in conflict
with trustworthy evidence that it must be set down as
fable.[142]   Isocrates did not look upon the battle as an
unmixed evil, but as a final clash between the ambitions of individual states to be free to quarrel among
themselves and the larger purpose of Philip to unite
and lead them against Persia.[143]   Nor could he have
felt that Chaeronea was in any peculiar sense "fatal to
liberty"; for the downfall of "freedom and autonomy"
dates, not from this event, but from the Peace of Antalcidas, which not only surrendered Greek territory to
Persian rule but conceded the right of the Persian king

---

[140] See Holm, Vol. III, p. 280: "If the Greeks had honestly
thrown in their lot with Philip and Alexander in the spirit of
Isocrates, they would have reaped the advantage of victory over
Asia without the disadvantage of Macedonian rule over Greece."
[141] 10th sonnet.
[142] The third in our collection of letters, written to Philip after
the peace which followed the battle of Chaeronea, is now generally
accepted as genuine.
[143] Letter III, 2, 4.

to dictate the relations of the Greek states generally.[144]
Philip succeeded to the overlordship of a barbarian
despot; and Philip was at least a Greek who proposed
to champion Hellenism.

It would be interesting to know what Isocrates
thought when the Athenians, in gratitude for the generous terms of peace which Philip made with them
after his victory, elected him to citizenship and set up
his statue in the market place.[145] Isocrates, himself,
in the letter which he then wrote to him,—the last of
his compositions—speaks with a dignified reserve.
There is no longer need, he says, to talk of reconciling
the Greek states; they must now perforce submit to
your purpose. It remains for you not to neglect the
great cause but to carry it out. I do not know whether
I won you over to this purpose or whether you yourself conceived it and I merely supported you in your
desires; although I am inclined to think (he says
politely) that it was your idea from the first. But I
am grateful to my old age for this one thing—that I
have lived long enough to see the dreams which have
been in my mind from my youth, and which I have
tried to write down in the *Panegyricus* and in the address to you, now coming true in part through your
deeds, and destined, I hope, to come entirely true.

The question of the practical effect of Isocrates upon
the course of events in his time is a matter of con-

[144] See Isocrates *Paneg.*, especially 205; and Ferguson, *Hellenistic
Athens*, p. 6.
[145] Holm, *op. cit.*, III., p. 282.

troversy, the evidence being purely circumstantial. It has been almost a fashion since Niebuhr to divorce him entirely from history, and to dismiss him as a sort of dreamer in the desert. He was undoubtedly an idealist who was far in advance of his age; [146] but to deny that he had any shaping influence upon contemporary history is to impeach the judgment of antiquity. He exercised a strong influence through his school; he was an outstanding publicist whose writings were widely read throughout Greece; he was on terms of friendship with many of the leading men of his time; he was the chief advocate of the pan-Hellenic idea, and as such was the spokesman for a considerable group of thinking men. It is true that in the last words which he wrote he gives Philip credit for his resolution to captain the Greeks in a crusade against the barbarians, and assigns to himself the minor rôle of supporting Philip in his design; but if that statement is to be interpreted as anything more than a courteous compliment; if, that is to say, we take the view that the life work of Isocrates has no real connection with the enterprise which Philip undertook and Alexander carried out, then the close correspondence which exists between the rather definite program which Isocrates outlined in the *Panegyricus* and in the *Address to Philip* and the articles of confederation which were adopted at the

[146] See Bury II, p. 300; "Neither Demosthenes, the eloquent orator, nor Eubulus, the able financier, saw far into the future. The only man of the day, perhaps, who grasped the situation in its œcumenical aspect, who descried, as it were from without, the place of Macedonia in Greece and the place of Greece in the world, was the nonagenarian Isocrates." See also Holm, III, p. 159.

Congress of Corinth one year after the battle of Chaeronea, by which the Greek states bound themselves to unite in a war against Persia under the leadership of the King of Macedon, is the most remarkable coincidence of history.[147]

[147] For the articles of the treaty, see Grote, XI, p. 340; and for a detailed comparison of these articles with the program of Isocrates, see Kessler, *Isokrates und die pan-Hellenische Idee,* p. 73 ff.